# SENSE AND NONSENSE ABOUT HOTHOUSE CHILDREN

## A practical guide for parents and teachers

### Michael J A Howe

*Department of Psychology*
*University of Exeter*

First published in 1990 by BPS Books (The British Psychological Society), St Andrews House, 48 Princess Road East, Leicester, LE1 7DR.

**British Library Cataloguing in Publication Data**

Howe, Michael J.A. (Michael John Anthony)
Sense and Nonsense about Hothouse Children
1. Gifted children. Education
I. Title II. British Psychological Society
371.95

ISBN 1-85433-039-X

Printed and bound in Great Britain by BPCC Wheatons Ltd.
Whilst every effort has been made to ensure the accuracy of the contents of this publication, the publishers and authors expressly disclaim responsibility in law negligence or any other cause of action whatsoever.

# CONTENTS

Chapter One

# Hothousing: A Boon Or A Menace?

A young child has something in common with a visitor to an unfamiliar and exotic country. Seen for the first time, a new land appears stimulating, exciting, and richly interesting, but also deeply confusing. It is hard to make sense of what is going on. Plenty is happening, but its meaning and significance is not at all clear. We need a guide who is familiar with the country to explain things to us. We want somebody to draw our attention to what is important, to help us to understand the apparently incomprehensible language, to tell us how we can interpret what we see and show us what we need to learn. Without a guide we may never make sense of the information that bombards us. However rich and stimulating, we may fail to perceive it as more than a chaotic mass of meaningless impressions.

Parents are a child's first guides. They explain the world and make it comprehensible. As guides, some mothers and fathers do a marvellous job. They are endlessly patient, and sensitive to the particular needs, interests, and varying moods of their child. They are tireless in helping their child to notice whatever is most significant. They point out each new event, and encourage the child to attend to it. As well as simply being stimulated, the child is carefully guided. The child's attention is not directed randomly, but is focused selectively on those particular aspects of the perceived world that the parents judge to be important for equipping the child with knowledge and understanding.

Other parents are less effective. They may be just as keen to teach and explain, but not quite so sensitive to a child's moods. They may lack self-confidence, or be too preoccupied with other tasks or their own worries to give as much undiluted attention to the job of making the world comprehensible to their sons and daughters. Or they may fail to realize just how much a child's progress can benefit from the sensitivity, patience, and diligence of parents.

## HELPING CHILDREN TO MAKE PROGRESS

This book is mainly for parents, teachers and others who are concerned about the quality of the guidance that children are given, and their opportunities for learning, in the earliest years. It raises questions concerning what can and what should be done to help young children to progress by gaining the kinds of skill and knowledge that will give them an unusually good start in life. In particular, it examines the challenging claim that most young children are capable of moving ahead just as fast and just as far as that minority whose exceptional precocity is seen as being evidence of special gifts or talents.

There is a magazine cartoon in which a woman is standing on a beach. Out at sea a tiny figure can just be seen. The woman is waving her hands in distress. She shouts to the other people on the beach: 'Help, help! My son the Doctor is drowning!' The joke reminds us how fiercely interested many parents are in their children's achievements. All parents want their sons and daughters to do well. We hope that our children will enjoy lives that are interesting and fulfilling. The wish that one's children will grow up capable and resourceful is shared by every parent, not only those who are unusually competitive or ambitious, or determined that their offspring will become child prodigies at any cost.

So we encourage children to make the best of themselves. We try to make sure that they have a good start in life, and we do what we can to provide opportunities for them to gain useful skills and abilities. Most parents would agree that a young person who is competent and well educated, and also self-confident about coping with new challenges, will begin adult life with real advantages.

Yet it isn't enough for parents just to *want* to encourage their children to learn. Wishing to give a child more opportunities to master skills that enrich life is not the same as having the means to do so. Many adults feel that they lack the necessary expertise. No one was at all surprised by the finding of one recent study that children made more progress at reading if their parents were actively involved in their learning. What was surprising was that many of those parents who did *not* help their children to read were just as keen to do so as the others were, but felt helpless and frustrated because they had no idea where to begin. The sad thing is that there are plenty of highly effective activities which they could have engaged in to encourage their children and teach them essential reading skills, and many other precious abilities as well. But these parents did not know what to do. They lacked access to assistance that would have enabled them to give really effective help.

Lack of know-how is a major reason for parents doing far less than they might do to accelerate learning in their young children. There are other reasons as well. One is the belief, still shared by many adults, that a young person's achievements, especially ones that are at all unusual, depend upon gifts and talents that certain individuals are born possessing. Of course, if that were true there would be no point in making special efforts to give 'ordinary' children special opportunities for learning. But in fact, as we shall see, such a viewpoint is misguided.

A third inhibiting influence, for many people, is the thought that encouraging a child to develop faster or farther than average in certain directions might have undesirable side-effects. Perhaps the child will be subjected to unreasonable pressures. Perhaps exceptional early progress in one direction will have the effect of impeding other aspects of development that are equally vital, such as social or emotional growth. Unlike the other two reasons for holding back, this third one is entirely reasonable. There undoubtedly are grounds for being concerned about the possible side-effects of accelerated early learning. Some individuals with highly impressive abilities have never been able to take advantage of them because too narrow or too uneven an education has left them unprepared for life in the real world. John Stuart Mill's rueful remark that 'I never was a boy' reminds us that intensive early education, even when it has been remarkably successful, can leave scars as well. A productive and happy adult life may be ruled out for someone whose too-specialized early childhood education has left them emotionally retarded or incapable of forming friendships and getting along with others.

But although these concerns are certainly genuine, it would be a pity if they had the effect of dissuading parents from encouraging their children to engage in early learning activities. There are many ways in which early education can move ahead without causing any harm.

## HOTHOUSING: THE CLAIMS

Recently, some extremely strong claims have been put forward concerning the apparently beneficial effects of giving a child an early so-called 'hothouse' education. In a British documentary television series, *Hot House People*, viewers were told that all children should be 'programmed for genius' and that every child has a greater potential intelligence than Leonardo da Vinci ever used. They were also told that education should begin in the womb. Viewers were assured that any baby can acquire 'encyclopaedic knowledge'.

Many parents who are ambitious for their children have had their hopes and aspirations fuelled by claims like these. The publicity which greeted these assertions had one very positive outcome: it made people more aware just how much a child's progress as a learner might depend upon the ways in which parents and other adults act to provide opportunities and give encouragement. But the claims also intensified parents' concerns and anxieties. Many an adult has become more confused about raising children. Mothers and fathers worry: 'Am I doing enough to stimulate Mark?' 'Should I be spending more time on educating Sarah?'

Although the terms 'hothouse' and 'hothousing' have no universally agreed definitions, they broadly refer to efforts to raise young children in circumstances that provide intensive, structured, and relatively formal education. The word 'superbaby' is also frequently uttered, although it seems to lack a precise meaning. Advocates of hothousing recommend that intensive education should begin very early in life, preferably in the first year. The teaching is usually done by the parents, but typically with the aid of outside guidance and commercially prepared instructional materials. There is often an emphasis on specifically intellectual kinds of skills and knowledge.

Promoters of hothousing programmes are quick to point out that the learning capacity of young children is very great. They argue that few young children are given nearly enough learning opportunities to take full advantage of their capacity. As it happens, they are absolutely right on both these counts. But some of their assertions are more equivocal. For instance, it is often implied by hothousing enthusiasts that the greater the amount of intellectual stimulation that a young child receives, the better. That claim is questionable for two reasons. First, simply giving a child a stimulating environment is not enough to ensure that the child will gain the maximum benefit from it. Second, the experiences that enable a child to learn need to be appropriately timed or coordinated. Sometimes, new information can have a distracting influence, by preventing a child from concentrating on other experiences relevant to the acquisition of a new skill (White, 1971).

Just as questionable is another suggestion made by some hothousing enthusiasts, that a baby's education should begin in the womb. A California obstetrician who runs a so-called 'pre-natal university' is quoted as claiming that 'five hundred pre-natal university graduates have shown enhanced physical and mental development; pre-natal stimulation is said to lead to early speech, physical agility and healthy bonding. "They begin using sentences earlier," the doctor says' (Walmsley and Margolis, 1987, p. 68). In fact, there is no scientific evidence to justify these claims. That is not to deny that unborn infants may be sensitive to certain kinds of information provided by the environment. For instance, there is a fascinating report of an experiment in which pregnant women read extracts from a children's book, *The Cat in the Hat*, twice a day during the final six weeks of their pregnancies. Later, it was discovered that the infants preferred listening to *The Cat in the Hat* to hearing another poem read by the mother (Kolata, 1984). It is not entirely clear how this intriguing finding can be explained. It certainly raises the possibility that unborn infants may be capable of perceiving and retaining in memory certain kinds of auditory information. Yet, whatever the explanation, the finding does not justify the claims of those who assert that infant education must begin before birth.

Of course, it may well be true that babies who are stimulated in the womb do tend to become intelligent children. But if that is so, the most likely reason is that those parents who spend time stimulating a baby *before* birth also spend above-average amounts of time teaching their baby *after* birth.

As we shall see in Chapter 2, quite a number of the claims that have been made about the likely benefits of hothousing are supported by firm evidence. One thing that is clear is that many children are capable of gaining extremely impressive skills while they are still very young. A wealth of evidence points to this conclusion. Millions of viewers of the *Hot House People* series watched 2-year-olds reading, and 6-year-olds communicating with computers in various programming languages, playing musical instruments, and conversing (and reading) in a foreign language. One child is said to have learned to play chess by the age of 3. Other young children are remarkably competent at mathematical skills.

## FOUR STARTING POINTS

In this book we shall be looking at various claims and counter-claims, and trying to establish what is true and what is false, and what are the likely benefits and the possible dangers of parental teaching activities of one kind or another. The book takes a hard look at current knowledge concerning the outcomes of practical efforts to accelerate the early progress of young children. One of the aims of the book is to give practical advice for parents who want to encourage their young child to gain valuable skills and abilities considerably earlier than is usual.

At this early point I need to make four simple observations. All are backed by the findings of scientific research. All will reappear later in the book, accompanied by more detailed arguments or fuller documentation.

1 The vast majority of young children are definitely capable of learning many skills at an earlier age than is usual.

2 Virtually any literate parent can learn how to provide the kinds of opportunities and the stimulating experiences that are necessary. Parents do not need to have special or hard-to-acquire instructional skills. But that doesn't mean that teaching a child is effortless. It takes time, sensitivity and tact, a willingness to persevere, and, above all, patience.

3 So long as other circumstances are favourable, the absence of innate special gifts or talents will not make it impossible for any normal child to develop almost any skill to a high level. (As it happens, there are strong reasons for doubting whether innate gifts and talents exist at all.)

4 Parents do need to be sensible and realistic about what they are setting out to achieve. The sheer fact that is *possible* for a child to master a particular accomplishment earlier than is customary does not automatically make it *desirable* for the child to do so. Any parent who plans, as some have done, to 'make my child a genius' will probably fail to achieve that goal, and quite possibly make it difficult for the child to enjoy a happy and productive life.

## EXAMINING THE HOTHOUSING CLAIMS

Some demonstrations of the remarkable feats performed by young children who have been exposed to hothousing regimes are unquestionably impressive. On their own, such demonstrations cannot provide conclusive proof that hothousing is as effective as it is claimed to be, but they certainly appear to support the assertion that the children's special abilities are the outcome of special early education.

It is highly unlikely that the majority of the young children who many people saw performing so impressively in the television series have been specially endowed with any rare innate talents or natural 'gifts'. The fact that in most cases the parents did not possess any remarkable abilities, and nor did other relatives who were not given intensive teaching in early childhood, casts doubt on an explanation based on the idea that some children are born with special genetic advantages. Although there is no firm evidence to confirm the assertion that *any* child is capable of making extraordinary progress at an early age, if only there are enough opportunities to learn and enough encouragement, it is clear that the potential positive effects of hothousing are not confined to a small minority of children.

Undoubtedly, we can find plenty that is wrong or ridiculous in the hothousing advocates' assertions, and there is much to be concerned about in some of their recommendations. But the core idea that most children have a much greater capacity to learn than most of us realize – and are therefore capable of achieving far more than the majority of children actually do – cannot be dismissed out of hand, and deserves to be seriously investigated.

Human abilities are a valuable natural resource. Outstanding skills and accomplishments are especially precious, if only because the exceptional achievements of a small number of individuals can benefit millions of others. So, quite apart from our desire to help our own children to make the best of their lives, we cannot afford to be indifferent to the possibility – which the promoters of hothouse education have pressed upon our attention – that the capabilities of every child can be greatly increased.

Yet it is all too clear that we must be wary of any approach that can harmfully interfere with an individual's childhood. Young children are highly vulnerable. Any kind of pressure to specialize at certain activities may have undesirable effects. At best, a child may be deprived of opportunities for relaxing, watching television, and playing with others. Ostensibly, activities like these may not have enormous value, but in fact they provide many occasions for a young person to gain social skills and learn how people can deal with their feelings. From activities like these the child gains numerous items of information that contribute to life in the everyday world. At worst, a child whose intensive early education in particular intellectual skills and narrow forms of knowledge leads to the loss of opportunities to interact with other children, to learn how to make friends, share experiences with others, gain a sense of humour, may never succeed in becoming a mature and independent adult. Such individuals may fail to acquire the capacity to make personal choices and decisions or to look after themselves properly, and never gain any real sense of direction or understand their own emotional needs.

So it is hardly surprising that parents' reactions to the various claims that have been made on behalf of hothousing approaches are somewhat mixed. On the one hand there is intense interest and excitement, coupled with a concern that they themselves may be failing to do all they could be doing to help and encourage their children to gain vital human skills. But on other hand there is also considerable suspicion about the validity of some of the claims. And this is combined with the fear that hothousing regimes, while they may well have desirable outcomes, may also have a damaging influence on children.

The result is that many parents have become thoroughly confused. They are pulled in two opposite ways. The potential importance of what is being asserted seems too great to ignore, but it is hard to decide how best to react. There seem to be too few hard facts and too many doubts and unanswered questions.

## THE AIMS OF THE BOOK

My aim, so far as the current state of knowledge permits, is to reduce parents' uncertainty and confusion about hothousing and early learning, and everything those terms imply. I shall examine evidence that helps to answer the various questions that parents and others have raised concerning a number of important practical issues. Most of the questions fall into one or more of the following three broad categories.

First, there are questions about the effectiveness of various procedures designed to promote increased learning or accelerated early development. They address the issues raised by a parent who asks 'What can be done to help my young child to make good progress?'

Second, there are questions about the desirability of taking various kinds of action that are designed to promote learning in a young child. These are the queries raised by parents who are rightly concerned about the possible damaging effects of hothousing methods. Such questions bring to the surface parents' fears that some approaches may be too intensive, too structured, too formal, or too specialized. These questions are relevant to the concerns of the parent who asks 'What *should* I do to encourage my child?'

Third, there are many down-to-earth questions about practical ways in which parents can make opportunities for helping children to learn. These are the questions of the parent who asks '*How can I put into practice* my intentions to encourage my young child to learn more?'

Each chapter addresses questions from one or more of those three categories. Chapter 2 looks at some of the findings of research that has been undertaken in order to discover just how effective are various procedures that have been designed to help young children to acquire important skills and abilities earlier than they are normally gained. The research findings show us what it is actually possible to achieve, and what works best. The chapter identifies ways in which parental encouragement and teaching can lead to a child's progress being successfully brought ahead.

Chapter 3 considers the possible side-effects. It looks at the likely outcomes of approaches to child-raising in which the parents place an unusual degree of emphasis on the acquisition of particular skills and abilities at an early age. It discusses the effects of a child being subjected to pressures of one kind or another. It considers some of the different normal childhood experiences through which young people gain intellectual, social, and practical abilities (and various attributes and habits as well) that enable them to take a full part in the adult world. Chapter 3 then examines certain of the ways in which intensive early education may disrupt these experiences, or even deprive a child of opportunities that are necessary elements of education for adult life.

Chapter 4 is the first of a group of three chapters that deal with the strictly practical issues confronting parents who wish to put into practice their intentions to encourage children to gain new abilities. These chapters introduce some of the nuts and bolts of early childhood learning. Chapter 4 includes a number of down-to-earth guidelines for adults who are keen to teach their children.

Chapter 5 is about the parent's role in helping a child to master language. Although virtually all children gain language without any formal instruction being necessary, efforts by parents to encourage language development can and do make an enormous difference. Even in infancy, opportunities that parents can make available will have beneficial effects. This and the next chapter include practical advice about methods and procedures for helping children to learn new skills. Numerous learning games and exercises for parent and child to enjoy together are described.

Chapter 6 introduces practical plans, methods, and games for helping a child to gain skills that will help make reading possible. Many of the difficulties that some children experience in learning to read at school are caused by a lack of basic language-related abilities. These are readily acquired at home, if a child is encouraged to enjoy books and to become interested in and aware of the letters and sounds that are experienced in written language.

Chapters 7 and 8 examine various aspects of the lives of exceptionally able young people. Chapter 7 looks at evidence concerning the background factors that nourish exceptional abilities. It describes some interview-based research that examined circumstances in which young people who had gained outstanding accomplishments began to develop their special interests and started gaining extraordinary skills. The findings challenge the popular notion that those individuals who gain extraordinary achievements must be inherently different from ordinary people.

Child prodigies – and the practical lessons we can draw from them – are the subject of Chapter 8. Some of these individuals have eventually become leading figures of their times; others have been less successful in later life. In a few instances, individuals who were brilliant prodigies in childhood never adapted to adulthood at all successfully. The chapter looks into the circumstances that give rise to child prodigies, and examines some of the problems they experience.

In Chapters 9 and 10 I take a critical look at some of the ways in which people customarily think about exceptional abilities and the causes underlying them. Our thoughts about the nature of abilities has influenced our policies towards encouraging and promoting them, sometimes in negative and unhelpful ways. Chapter 9 takes a broader look at the causes of outstanding human abilities. It shows how some of the ways in which we perceive exceptional people actually impede our efforts to understand how and why people differ. In particular, most adults fail to appreciate the extent to which a person's specific abilities can thrive separately, largely independently of the same individual's level of competence in other areas. This chapter also examines the concept of intelligence, which has powerfully shaped our views about the nature and causes of human abilities. I suggest that much current thinking about intelligence is mistaken, and presents serious practical obstacles to progress.

Chapter 10 looks at the roles of genetic and hereditary causes in determining people's ability levels, an area of knowledge that many people find confusing. Contrary to what is often supposed, hereditary influences do not affect abilities in a fixed, direct, or all-or-none fashion. A common fallacy is the assumption that if inherited influences are crucial, then environmental factors must be unimportant. Chapter 10 also examines confusions that arise from the ways in which many people use words that are believed to denote causes of high abilities. It looks at some of the ways in which babies differ at birth, and examines possible mechanisms via which early differences can influence subsequent abilities.

Chapter Two

# Can Children's Development
# Be Accelerated?

There is no point in making efforts to accelerate a child's early progress unless it is possible to be reasonably certain that those efforts will have the desired effect. It is not inconceivable that a young child will be simply incapable of acquiring certain kinds of abilities until a certain chronological age is reached. According to one view, for instance, a child might be unable to read until a stage of age-related physiological readiness is achieved. So it is clear that we ought not to take it for granted that intensive learning procedures will actually work. Do they or don't they?

In principle, it should not be too difficult for researchers to carry out experiments designed to measure the effectiveness of attempts to promote learning in babies and young children. But the necessary long-term intensive research programmes are expensive. Largely for that reason, although research investigations have produced many interesting findings, the evidence is in many ways incomplete. That is to say, the research findings do not provide unambiguous answers to all the significant questions about the effectiveness of efforts to promote early learning. And there are very few recent investigations which provide anything like a satisfactory direct test of the assertions that have made by those who favour hothousing approaches to education in early childhood.

## A NATURAL EXPERIMENT

Occasionally, we discover that important questions can be answered without it being necessary to undertake any new research studies at all. One such question is that of whether or not 'ordinary' children are capable of gaining exceptional musical skills. Is that possible? Or are exceptional musical accomplishments possible only for a child who has been fortunate enough to be born with a special musical aptitude or talent? As it happens, a rather convincing answer has been supplied by historical information about some events that took place almost three hundred years ago.

In Venice, at the beginning of the eighteenth century, there were a number of orphanages in which music was very highly valued. The composer Antonio Vivaldi worked at one of these orphanages, 'la Pietà', where he taught violin-playing to the orphan girls. At la Pietà the young orphans heard regular musical concerts and had many opportunities to receive musical training. They were also strongly encouraged to become accomplished performers or singers, and many reached levels of performance that were universally admired. Visitors to Venice at that time flocked to attend the concerts given at la Pietà, where new works by Vivaldi and other composers were regularly performed. It was said that the quality of the orphans' concerts was unsurpassed anywhere in the world (Koldener, 1970; Kunkel, 1985).

These remarkable achievements occurred despite the fact that many of the orphan girls at la Pietà came from backgrounds of squalor and destitution. So, assuming for the moment that there is some truth in the idea that certain individuals are naturally endowed with musical gifts that are genetically transmitted within a family, it is unlikely that so many of the orphans of la Pietà would have been blessed in that manner. Nevertheless, as we have seen, by the time they reached adolescence, a substantial proportion of the orphan girls – perhaps a third of them – had become exceptionally skilled young musicians.

Looking back to these musical happenings at la Pietà, we can regard them as forming a kind of unplanned experiment. It seems to contradict the view that outstanding musical skills can be gained only by those fortunate individuals who have inherited an innate talent for music. It suggests that when there exists an environment which values musical accomplishments and gives individuals rich opportunities to learn musical skills, it may not be necessary to have a special innate aptitude in order to reach high levels of expertise.

# ACCELERATING PHYSICAL ABILITIES

Normally, of course, we cannot rely on the existence of natural experiments for deciding on the truth or falsity of claims concerning the effectiveness of training in early childhood. It is usually necessary to undertake experimental research studies. Some particularly interesting ones were done between the two world wars. At that time Arnold Gesell carried out an interesting series of infant training experiments. For instance, in a study that is frequently cited in psychology textbooks, one of a pair of identical twin girls was given instruction in a variety of skills, including six weeks' training at climbing stairs (Gesell and Thompson, 1929). The training began when she was 46 weeks of age. The other twin received no instruction in stair-climbing until seven weeks later.

The design of this experiment made it possible for Gesell to test the effectiveness of the early training that one of the twins received. Gesell's own view was that human development is largely a process of 'unfolding'. He argued that there is no point in trying to teach young children new skills until they reach a stage of 'readiness', which comes as a result of naturally-occurring physical maturation. According to him, efforts to accelerate early progress would have no long-term beneficial effects at all. Consequently, he did not expect the twin who was trained earlier to do better than the other twin, at least in the long run.

At first sight his results seemed to confirm this. Gesell reported that the initial advantage gained by the specially trained child was wiped out after the other twin had been trained for just two weeks, beginning seven weeks later. But as William Fowler (1983) discovered after a careful re-examination of Gesell's findings, there is clear evidence that the early training did after all produce substantial and permanent advantages. In follow-up studies, the twin who was trained first continued to do better at the majority of the skills she had been taught. When they were teenagers, the twin who had received the early training was still superior to the other twin at a number of abilities, such as walking, tap-dancing, and running. And even at adolescence, the twin who had been taught earlier was ahead on a number of language skills.

It is also interesting to note that not only was the progress of the twin who received special early training well ahead of the average, but so too was that of the other twin, who was also given special training, but later. For instance, after receiving less than five hours' instruction in climbing stairs, the second twin could climb five stairs on her own. At this time she was just a year old. For comparison, the average child cannot walk up stairs until around 18 months. Had Gesell been less blinkered by his certainty that everything depends upon physical maturation, he would not have failed to notice the significance of the fact that even the later-trained twin was well ahead of the developmental norms.

The long-term benefits that were observed seem especially impressive when we remember that the special training was brief in duration and not at all intensive. We might expect that a lengthier intervention would have even stronger effects. In some research investigations conducted by Myrtle McGraw (1935, 1939), one fraternal twin, named Johnny, received training in a number of physical skills between the ages of 7 months and 24 months, five days per week. The other twin (Jimmy) also received intensive training, but it was delayed until he was 22 months of age, and much less prolonged. The effects were large and permanent. Johnny, whose training was more prolonged, was well ahead of Jimmy on all the skills taught, and his progress was much above average. He swam on his own at 10 months, and at 15 months he could dive from the side of a swimming pool. At about the same age he dived straight into a lake that he was visiting for the first time, and he could move on roller skates and climb steep slopes. When the twins were 6 years old, Johnny was still ahead of Jimmy. He displayed more coordination at most physical tasks, and he was much better at running, climbing, jumping, walking, swimming, and riding a tricycle. And even when they were both adults, aged 22, Johnny was more confident and more skilled at physical activities.

These findings show that reasonably intensive and long-lasting interventions can produce substantial early gains. And the advantages are certainly not just temporary ones. Recent research studies have yielded similar findings. For instance, 4-year-olds made large improvements over a fifteen-week period in another study, conducted by Fowler and his colleagues (Fowler et al., 1983). Every week the children were given three thirty-minute training sessions in gymnastic skills. By the end of the training period they had made no less than five times as much progress as normally occurs over a comparable period.

## CAN LANGUAGE BE ACCELERATED?

Taken as a whole, findings such as these make a strong case for the view that intensive early training can lead to substantial and long-lasting acceleration of physical skills. But does the same apply to intellectual abilities? This is not something that can be taken for granted.

Take the case of linguistic abilities. It is known that the vast majority of children acquire language naturally, even in the absence of any deliberate instruction. They do not seem to need to be taught language. In fact, deliberate teaching can have the outcome of impeding language development rather than accelerating it. Katherine Nelson discovered that children whose mothers rewarded them for pronouncing words correctly and punished them for poor pronunciation made *less* progress than children whose mothers were relatively unconcerned about correct pronunciation (Nelson *et al.*, 1973).

That finding suggests that efforts by parents to accelerate children's language development are likely to be counter-productive, perhaps even damaging. In that case, the wisest course might be to resist interfering with children's language development. There are other reasons for reaching this conclusion. First, the account of language acquisition put forward by Noam Chomsky, indicating that human brains must be innately wired up in particular ways in order for it to be possible for the young of our species to become competent at using language, seems to imply that the brain's physical development imposes firm limits on the age at which a child's language development can begin. Second, Jean Piaget's influential stage theory of human development indicates that there are major restrictions on the extent to which training can successfully extend young children's thinking abilities.

Not surprisingly, therefore, a common view among parents is that although it may be possible, with intensive early training, to accelerate the acquisition of *some* skills, the development of language, and perhaps that of certain other fundamental human abilities as well, simply cannot be accelerated. Attempts to speed up the learning of them are, it would appear, simply a waste of time. We should leave things alone, apparently.

Nevertheless, a few researchers have stubbornly persisted in undertaking research studies aimed at attempting to accelerate young children's acquisition of intellectual abilities, including language skills. Their findings are quite surprising, especially to those who have believed that such efforts are unlikely to have long-lasting beneficial effects.

One series of studies followed the language progress of fifteen babies who were taught by their parents from around 5 months of age (Fowler *et al.*, 1983). The parents were shown how to make use of a graduated language-learning programme. It started with activities designed to teach single-word referents for objects and actions, and gradually progressed to complex parts of speech and grammatical forms. Typically, the language stimulation took place in the context of informal play activities and social interactions which parents and children enjoyed. The parents were given a training manual and lists of words. To help some of the less well-educated, the experimenters also distributed picture books.

Most of the language activities in the programme were not very different from ones that many parents spontaneously initiate when they interact with their babies and young children. However, the activities took place more regularly and frequently than usual, involved a larger proportion of the time available, began when the baby was considerably younger than usual, and were systematic, consistent, and systematically graduated. The babies' progress was carefully recorded. In order to help assess the effects of the programme, the investigators also observed the progress of some other infants, of similar ages, who received no special instruction.

The results were impressive. At the age of one year, four of the fifteen infants who were given special training were speaking in sentences. (That achievement does not usually occur until about the twentieth month.) Three of the infants were using five-word sentences by 20 months, and by 24 months almost all were doing so. (The usual age for this is 32 months.) The trained children began to use pronouns at 18 months on average (compared with the norm of 23 months), self-referral pronouns such as 'I' and 'me' at 18 months (compared with 29 months), and plurals before 24 months (compared with the 34-month norm). On a test that was designed to measure children's language skills, the Griffiths Language Test, their scores at the beginning of the study were around the average, but after six months they were 40 per cent higher than the (near-average) scores achieved by the children in the control group.

The effects were long-lasting, as well. Those children whose parents continued to record their progress maintained their superiority at using language until they were at least 5 years old (the final occasion on which they were tested). The language skills of those children in the study whose families were less formally educated, and placed little value on highly structured language, tended to dip towards the average as they got older. All the same, when the final tests were administered, even the children of the least educated families stayed well above the norms.

Interestingly, the sole middle-class family in which the initial advantages disappeared was one in which the mother decided to discontinue giving stimulation when her son was a year old. She told the researchers she wanted to be sure that the boy would not be different from other children. Six months later, his language-quotient score and his IQ score had each dropped by over thirty points.

These findings demonstrate that intensive language stimulation in early infancy can have large and persisting positive effects after all. At least one other study has provided additional evidence that intensive language stimulation can have outcomes of this impressive degree of magnitude. J. McVicker Hunt, working with foundlings in an orphanage in Tehran, found that intensive special language stimulation, which started when the infants were just 4 weeks old and was given by caregivers who had been trained in language-acquisition techniques that placed stress on verbal interactions, had enormous positive effects. By the time they were 2 years of age, the children had not only progressed dramatically faster than other children brought up in the conditions of the orphanage, but equalled the language achievements of children brought up in professional families in the United States (Hunt, 1986).

The results of a more recent investigation show that even relatively brief language training, of just one month's duration, can produce substantial and long-lasting advantages. In a study by Whitehurst *et al.* (1988), middle-class parents were taught to give their children (aged between 21 months and 35 months) more encouragement to talk, and better feedback, when they were reading to them from picture books. The parents were trained to encourage children to talk about the contents of the pictures, rather than passively listening and looking. Parents were also told to ask 'What?' questions (for example, 'There's Eeyore. What's happening to him?'), designed to help a child to participate actively. They were also encouraged to give the children informative feedback, and instructed to make progressive changes in the form of their interventions and their play with the child. Reading sessions were taped, so that the experimenters could measure the degree to which the training was actually implemented. To measure longer-term effects of the programme, the children were tested again nine months after the initial one-month period.

There was a substantial positive outcome. At the end of the one-month training period, the thirty trained children were eight months ahead of subjects who formed a control group (whose parents read to them equally often) on the Illinois Test of Psycholinguistic Abilities, and six months ahead on another test, the Expressive One-Word Picture Vocabulary Test. Nine months later, the children in the experimental group were still six months ahead of the other children.

It is noteworthy that this dramatic improvement occurred despite the fact that the programme required only one hour of direct training for the parents. These findings indicate that there is much scope for acceleration in most children's language development. It is clear that the customary reading behaviours of parents, even highly motivated and affluent ones who spend hours every week reading to their children, are not nearly so effective as they could be.

Other studies investigating the outcomes of relatively modest and short-term language interventions have yielded findings that are equally dramatic, and broadly similar to the ones I have described. In one experiment, 2-year-olds made substantial gains in language skills following instruction totalling no more than five hours in duration (Nelson, 1977). In yet another study there was a similar improvement in early language skills in considerably younger children as a result of language stimulation after their parents had received guidance, in sessions totalling no more than ninety minutes, in the use of simple vocalization and labelling activities (Metzl, 1980). Guiding the parents in this manner led to marked language improvements in babies in each of three age groups, 6 weeks, 12 weeks, and 18 weeks, and follow-up studies administered several years later showed that the children's above-average progress was maintained.

Other research studies have confirmed that the responsiveness of mothers to their children's own utterances affects language development (Petersen and Sherrod, 1982). And researchers have observed improvements in language skills when appropriate social or material rewards are given to normal infants as young as 6 months (Staats, 1971). In a study by P.W. Drash and A.L. Stolberg (cited by Fowler, 1990) it was found that a more intensive intervention programme, in which parents were given training and guidance for three hours each week over a seven-month period, aimed at teaching language skills and other abilities to their (initially) 6-month-old infants, had very striking positive effects. Following the intervention, the children's scores on tests of language development were much above the average, and so were their scores on tests of general intelligence. Moreover, follow-up studies, the final one of which was administered when the children were 3 years and 6 months, showed that the children's advantages were maintained with no diminution.

One especially important finding is that the appropriateness of the speech that is directed to a child is far more crucial than the sheer amount of it. The most effective kinds of language teaching occur when an adult and a child are together in a one-to-one situation, and the adult knows what is momentarily engaging the child's attention. Children are more likely to learn the name of an object from an adult when the child is already expressing an interest in the object than when the mother has to draw the child's attention to it (Hart and Risley, 1980; Valdez-Menchaca and Whitehurst, 1988; White, 1985).

In short, the evidence that has emerged from research investigations proves that children's acquisition of basic language skills can be substantially accelerated. The effects of such acceleration can be long-lasting. And, as the findings reported by Whitehurst and his co-researchers make clear, it is not just those children whose early language environments are unusually impoverished who stand to gain from being given improved opportunities to learn. It is quite possible, as Fowler (1990) suggests, that with appropriate language stimulation virtually all children are capable of progressing far beyond the levels of language ability that are now considered to be normal.

Because language plays such a crucial part in human life, not only as a vehicle for communicating with others but also as a tool that fundamentally affects the ways in which we humans think, the real effects of accelerating a child's language development are likely to be quite staggering. Language shapes our mental activities; it does not just reflect or communicate them. Language, thinking, and communicative skills are closely dependent on each other. Many of the everyday thoughts and cognitions that adults take for granted are inconceivable in the absence of language. Consequently, accelerating a child's linguistic progress has the inevitable outcome of extending that child's knowledge and understanding of the world. And since it is now clear that even those studies which involve only a small amount of time spent in helping parents to use simple techniques designed to extend children's use and understanding of language can be remarkably effective, there is absolutely no reason to delay encouraging more parents to engage in everyday play activities which promote language growth in infants and young children.

As Fowler (1990) points out, intensive early language stimulation plays a vital role in developing the kinds of excellence that are reflected in high scores on intelligence tests and in other measures of academic competence. Even mathematical abilities seem to benefit from intensive early verbal stimulation. And the chances are that if *all* parents made an effort to spend more time encouraging their young children's language development, the average level of competence at language-based skills would rise appreciably, bringing with it widespread increases in levels of performance at the many important capabilities and accomplishments to which language contributes.

# EARLY READING

A related intellectual skill, which if not quite so crucial as language itself is nonetheless extremely important, is reading. As well as providing a way of gaining access to knowledge, reading strongly influences the ways in which we use language. As a result, our thinking abilities are also extended.

Because most of us have been reading for as long as we can remember, we often fail to realize that only literate people understand certain very simple facts about language. Even the concept of a word has no precise meaning for an illiterate person. So when a child becomes able to read, more is gained than access to information: the child gains membership of a broad culture of literacy.

Everyone knows that some children learn to read earlier than others. Why does that happen? And is *any* normal child capable of learning to read well before the usual age?

Proud parents have sometimes been known to proclaim that their child learned to read entirely without help. If fact, that never happens. It is simply not possible to learn to read without assistance. At the very least, you need someone to tell you what the various symbols represent, and you need some kind of informative guidance or feedback to tell you whether you are on the right track. Children who gain the ability to read considerably earlier than usual have almost always had many opportunities to enjoy reading-related interactions with adults. There may not have been any formal instruction, but the child will almost certainly have had the opportunity to learn to enjoy books and to identify letter sounds. That child will have had enough exposure to the written word to gain a real *desire* to read.

Learning to read is not easy. It involves acquiring and then combining a number of different skills. It is not at all surprising that some children find it difficult. In reality, the remarkable thing is how few children *don't* learn how to read. It is curious that most people do not find it nearly so surprising that some individuals have trouble with learning other skills, such as driving a car, although the demands on the learner may be considerably lighter than the ones a child has to confront in the course of learning to read. There is no sound reason why with reading, unlike driving and other skills, people should find it necessary to invent special labels (such as 'dyslexic' or 'reading-disabled') for those children who experience difficulties.

As early as 1931, Helen Davidson described the findings of a large-scale experiment which she carried out in order to measure the effects of giving special training in reading to a number of young children, including a group of five 3-year-olds. Each child received no more than around six hours of formal instruction in all, in ten-minute individual daily lessons, spread over a period of four months. Although the training approach adopted was unusually 'child-centred' for the time, most of the elements are recognizable in today's methods of reading instruction. There were no special gimmicks.

Davidson found that even this relatively small amount of special instruction led to the 3-year-olds making very substantial progress. At the end of the study a child could recognize, on average, more than 120 printed words. The children's reading skills equalled those of average children two years older. One of the five was reading as well as an average 8-year-old, and two more had reading abilities equivalent to those of 7-year-olds who had received at least a year of schooling.

There were also some older children in Davidson's study. Not all of them did so well as the 3-year-olds. Her explanation is that the older children were not so intelligent, and she implies that only those children who are brighter than average can profit from being given instruction at a very early age. But Davidson's descriptions of the children and their families make it clear that the more successful children in her study were different from the others not only in having higher intelligence-test scores. The children who did well had parents who were better educated, who read to their sons and daughters more often, and who read more themselves. The probable reason for the 3-year-olds making better progress than some of the older children is suggested by Davidson's report that all but one of the former were read to regularly by their parents, whereas all but one of the latter were read to only occasionally.

Causes and effects are hard to separate in a study such as this one. The findings do not entirely rule out the possibility that early reading is available only to those young children who do well at intelligence tests. However, one researcher, Arthur Staats (1971), who describes the results of a small-scale study designed to teach reading skills, included among his subjects a boy aged 4 who came from a culturally deprived home environment and whose IQ was only 89. The instructional programme involved around seventeen hours in all. It consisted of a large number of very short sessions of around six minutes each. Despite the boy's disadvantages, by the end of the study he had gained reading and writing skills that were advanced for his age. In addition, his progress was not noticeably slower than that of another child of comparable age whose IQ was 130. These findings indicate that high measured intelligence is not essential for early reading. The majority of children are probably capable of learning to read at least a year or two earlier than the usual age. In most cases, early advantages in reading are maintained into later childhood and beyond (Durkin, 1966; Fowler, 1983).

It has been suggested that early reading can have negative effects on a child. If that were true, the advantages of learning to read earlier than usual might be outweighed by other factors. But in fact, no adverse effects at all have been observed in any of the studies that have compared early readers with other children. A study by E. Scott and B. Bryant (cited by Fowler, 1983) found early readers to be more independent and purposive than others, and just as sociable. And Fowler (1990) found that in a sample of twenty-one exceptionally intelligent children, virtually all of them learned to read unusually early. Their parents viewed language acquisition and reading not as ends in themselves but as doors to opportunities for gaining knowledge and mastering intellectual skills. None of these children gained their reading abilities in a vacuum: in every case the parents gave much attention to stimulating their child with language experiences and exposing them to books. The parents were energetic in talking to their child from infancy onwards, in drawing attention to the words for the objects and events a child was experiencing, and doing all they could to extend their child's vocabulary and increase understanding of the meaning of words. The parents were also keen to explain things and to encourage and answer their child's questions.

## CONCLUSION

Is it true that virtually every young child is capable of reaching the very highest levels of achievement in any sphere of ability? That is not an easy question to answer, and the evidence currently available does not provide firm grounds for either proving or falsifying the assertion. But research findings do give very firm support to the more modest claim that the development of young children's basic skills, such as language and reading, can be accelerated very substantially. Again and again, the research results demonstrate that it is quite possible for most young children to gain important abilities much earlier than usual. And when they do, the advantages are likely to be long-lasting.

Chapter Three

# Hothousing and Accelerated Learning: What are the Snags and Dangers?

The finding that parental tuition can be highly effective is a necessary condition for many parents deciding to stimulate early learning in young children; but it is not a sufficient condition. Before taking action it is still necessary to decide whether or not it is *wise* to encourage a child to gain basic skills earlier than usual.

As well as the positive effects of early training, there may also be negative ones. We need to be aware of the possible dangers. Forcing young people's growth into particular directions can have the effect of depriving them of valuable childhood experiences or restricting their opportunities to learn other things. We need to be certain that our efforts to help are doing more than simply equipping children with particular narrow abilities. It is vital to ensure that our efforts to accelerate the development of a child's skills will genuinely contribute to the overall quality of the child's future life.

In one of the films in the television series *Hot House People* the viewer meets an American family in which both parents have gone to enormous lengths to accelerate and extend the education of each of their four daughters. It is obvious that the parents' efforts have been remarkably successful. All the girls are unquestionably bright, and they are all well ahead of their peers at school. At the time the series was made the oldest daughter was 16, but already studying for her Ph.D. The second daughter, aged 13, was an undergraduate studying for her first degree. The third, at 11 years, was in a school class in which the other students were mostly aged 15 or 16. The youngest daughter, at 9 years of age, was also in a classroom where most of the other pupils were considerably older.

At one point in the film the oldest daughter, the brilliant 16-year-old, is quizzed about her hopes and aspirations for the future:

Asked 'Do you have great ambitions? Would you like to contribute something that's really important?' Susan told us: 'Not really. I guess it would be nice, but I don't really want to spend the rest of my life chasing after the hope that I can make a great contribution . . . my main goal in life is just to get married and have children.' (Walmsley and Margolis, 1987, p. 64)

I was puzzled when I first encountered these rather prosaic comments by a young person who possesses outstanding intellectual abilities. On reflection, my reaction to her words is ambivalent. On the one hand it comes as something of a relief that the girl appears to be such an ordinary 16-year-old. Despite having experienced an extraordinary childhood she clearly has not turned into the kind of robot-like thinking-machine that hothousing regimes are sometimes suspected of producing. On the other hand it seems rather sad that, after such great pains have been taken to enable this individual to gain exceptional skills, she appears to have no exciting plans to make use of them.

It is hard to imagine Marie Curie or Margot Fonteyn calmly asserting that their main goal in life was to get married and have children. People like them have aims, purposes, and a clear sense of direction that sets them far apart from this young lady. They know what they want to do with their lives. One gets the impression that, although the parents' efforts to give their daughter a superior education have succeeded in producing a child whose intellectual skills are extraordinarily advanced, the child has failed, up to now, to gain certain attributes that people must have in order to make productive use of their abilities. These other attributes are not specifically intellectual ones. They are more closely related to personality and temperament, and they underlie a person's curiosity, self-motivation, commitment, and self-confidence. But for equipping an individual to attain outstanding achievements, they may be just as vital as purely cognitive qualities are.

Perhaps I am expecting too much. Maybe it is unreasonable to expect that a 16-year-old, even an extraordinarily accomplished one, will necessarily share the precocious awareness that the young Einstein had of the direction he intended his career to take. Yet her reactions to the interviewer do raise issues which ought not to be ignored. A particularly important one is the fact that no significant human achievement depends upon intellectual qualities alone. If only for that reason alone, quite apart from broader humane concerns about individuals' mental health and happiness, it is essential to make sure that any intensive early educational regime which places special emphasis on a child's gaining knowledge and skills does not have the side-effect of reducing the child's opportunities to enjoy experiences that contribute to social, emotional, and moral growth.

## AMBITIOUS PARENTS

It is not easy to draw a line between conscientious parents, who are understandably keen to encourage their child to do well, and parents whose determination that their children will be successful makes a reasonably carefree childhood impossible and threatens the child's future happiness. Many parents think they 'know what is good for' their sons and daughters, but parents are often mistaken about this. Even the most sensitive and self-aware parents can be too ambitious for their children, and consequently self-deceiving, especially in matters that are as close to their hearts as the progress of their own flesh and blood. Much as we quite properly identify with our children, we have to remember that they are other people. They have their own lives to lead and their own goals and ambitions to decide on.

My own research into child prodigies suggests that certain problems are prone to occur in the rather close, intense, inward-looking family backgrounds that a number of intellectually precocious children have experienced. (Some of the problems and difficulties experienced by child prodigies will be discussed later, in Chapter 8.) Sometimes, parents start to live their own lives through the child, to the extent that the child's successes are vicariously experienced as victories for the parent. A possible reason for this is that the parents' own early hopes have been frustrated. When an adult is unhealthily keen to shape a young person's future destiny, the growing child's natural wish for independence from parental control may be seen as a rejection. Very often, family circumstances in which children appear to be over-dependent on their parents are in fact ones in which strong dependencies operate in both directions: parents and children are mutually over-dependent (Howe, 1990).

## GAINING SPECIAL SKILLS: THE COSTS TO A CHILD

Any parent who is trying to decide whether or not to give special encouragement to a young child to gain new abilities would be wise to ask: 'What does the child stand to *lose*? What are the possible costs? Will the child be deprived of experiences that could be valuable?' Only if the answer to all such questions is negative is it unquestionably wise for the parent to proceed, and then only so long as it is clear that the child definitely wants to learn, enjoys doing so, and is not experiencing any kind of pressure or anxiety.

That is not to say that no encouragement to gain a new ability should ever be given unless it is absolutely certain that there will be no cost to the child at all. Acquiring expertise, especially when it is highly specialized, usually requires sacrifices of some kind. Many of today's leading younger musicians had little free time for playing games with others or watching television when they were children, but the majority of these individuals would agree that the expense was justified. Even so, parents need to exercise enormous care when they are considering whether a child should be encouraged to specialize in time-consuming activities that restrict opportunities for other kinds of experience. It is never easy to be sure where the young child's best interests lie.

What are the costs that may be incurred? I have already referred to one, the possibility of parents placing unreasonable pressures on their children, and being too demanding. Then there is the fact that simply being in any way extraordinary can create real problems for a child. Most children, however precocious or intellectually superior they are, like to have friends of their own age, and want to feel accepted by their peers. But ordinary children can be intolerant of those whom they perceive as being odd or peculiar.

Of course, a child with well-developed social skills ought to be able to handle any difficulties in being accepted by other children. But unfortunately, gaining such skills may be especially difficult for a child whose home life is unusual. For instance, if the parents' values and interests contrast with those of the families of a child's peers, there may be few opportunities for a child to enjoy interests that are shared with others. Having shared knowledge about and attitudes towards the world outside school makes life more enjoyable for any young person. Shared experiences serve to oil the wheels of social intercourse: they make it easier to form friendships. So the child who rarely watches television, for instance, will lack a useful point of human contact.

Joan Freeman (1990) points out that friends, especially in adolescence, can be the best part of a young person's life. Contact with friends of their own age gives opportunities for teenagers to interpret their experiences and gain feedback which helps them to develop a sense of who they are. She raises the unhappy possibility of a clever boy, at first admired as a 'little professor', developing into an adolescent who has failed to develop social skills and make long-lasting friendships and is 'on the way to a life of loneliness, peering down a microscope away from people and emotional comfort'.

The difficulties are likely to be intensified if an intellectually able child is placed in a class in which the other pupils are substantially older. It can be especially hard for a child to get on with others who are more socially mature and who place value on activities such as sports and games in which a younger student is likely to be at a disadvantage.

It would be wrong to assume that any young person who is at all different from others will suffer. On the whole, children, like adults, are attracted to competent individuals and accept them as leaders. But a parent should be aware that children who are unlike their peers in a number of different ways may find it hard to establish comfortable social relationships at school.

When a child makes unusually fast progress in one particular area of competence, a degree of specialization is usually involved. Specialization can cause problems of its own. One cause of difficulties is the fact that other people, including teachers, may fail to understand the extent to which particular skills can be acquired in isolation from other abilities. A child – or an adult – who is an outstanding chess player, or a brilliant musician, or excellent at mathematics, may have no more than average competence at other intellectual abilities. Adults who fail to recognize this sometimes form quite unrealistic expectations of an individual. They may assume, for instance, that a young person who is an exceptional mathematician will be socially and emotionally mature as well. Even professionals who work with highly able young people may underestimate the extent to which a child's abilities can be fragmentary and autonomous. Many able youngsters have run into troubles caused by other people's faulty belief that the child's special abilities will be matched by comparable superiority in quite different areas.

Specializing can also lead to other difficulties. Concentrating on one activity inevitably restricts the time available for doing other things. A child who devotes five hours every day to piano practice cannot also spend a great amount of time on mathematics or biology, or social and leisure activities. Of course, the leisure hours of most young children are not filled with events of great value, and for that reason the price to be paid by a child whose unfilled leisure time is less than average is often fairly small. All the same, it is not entirely negligible. Children do learn from leisure activities, even relatively 'passive' ones such as watching television and spending time with their friends. It would be wrong to think that time-filling specialized pursuits that curtail leisure time carry no disadvantages at all. But it is easy to exaggerate the problems, or get them out of perspective. Most of the difficulties I have mentioned are likely to arise only when a young child is encouraged by the parents to have a lifestyle very different from that of most other children. In reality, there is an enormous amount that parents can do to help children become more competent at a number of valuable skills without seriously interfering in any way with their usual activities, interests, games, enthusiasms, and friendships. It is only when parents decide to go well beyond giving the kinds of stimulation that help to give a child a good start in life, and strongly encourage a child to commit very substantial amounts of time to a specialized area of expertise, that the course of childhood is likely to become abnormal.

Of course, an abnormal childhood is not inevitably a bad childhood. But any parent who does have plans to push a young person into concentrating in one area of development would be wise to ponder on the following passage, which appears in the autobiography of the eminent mathematician Norbert Wiener. Although Wiener enjoyed a highly successful career, he was bitterly aware that the behaviour of his forceful and demanding parents had made it hard for him to develop into an independent adult person, and virtually impossible to become the self-assured and socially competent adult he would have liked to be. Wiener's words do not hide the intensity of his feelings:

> Let those who choose to carve a human soul to their own measure be sure that they have a worthy image after which to carve it, and let them know that the power of molding an emerging intellect is a power of death as well as a power of life. (Wiener, 1953, p. 136)

## ADULTS' DECISIONS AND CHILDREN'S LIVES

There are no hard-and-fast rules that specify the precise degree to which parents ought to give their children special tuition or encourage them to learn new skills. In this chapter I have drawn attention to a number of matters that a parent needs to consider, and I have mentioned a variety of the problems that may arise. But ultimately, parents always have to make their own decisions about bringing up children.

In making such decisions, the most important thing to keep in mind is that the possession of a range of special skills and abilities, however exceptional and impressive they are, is not enough to prepare a young individual for living a rich and productive life. Other qualities are just as crucial. The survival skills that any person requires are many and varied. They include empathy, imagination, a sense of humour, enthusiasm, sympathy for others, aesthetic awareness and the capability to respond to beauty, a whole range of moral attributes, and the capacity to experience various feelings and emotions and understand the needs of other people. Equally important are communicative skills, abilities that enable a person to establish and maintain friendships, as well as a number of social skills, including those mentioned earlier in this chapter.

None of these qualities and skills emerges by magic. They all have to be acquired, and they will not be acquired unless a young person's experiences include opportunities for learning them. And young people also have to discover how to make decisions for themselves. It is impossible for children to learn how to do that if they are not allowed to make their own mistakes and learn from their own experiences.

There is little merit in a childhood which equips an individual with some impressive skills but leaves them lacking many of the other qualities I have mentioned. In the following account, by a journalist who is describing an attempt to interview a young person with a remarkable specialized ability, one senses the possibility that some important human capacities may be absent:

> I asked, for example, if there had ever been a subject that she had found difficult. It provoked hours of discussion. 'What sort of question is that? I can't possibly answer it.' . . . I said it was a perfectly simple question of the kind asked every day by non-geniuses. 'No question is ever simple,' came the triumphant, if rather pat, chorus . . . It was the most taxing conversation I have ever had, and also among the least interesting, like a football match that is constantly stopped by the referee for technical infringement. (Stephen Pile, quoted in Walmsley and Margolis, 1987, p. 54)

Except in the world of Lewis Carroll, we expect individuals to be capable of responding to people's questions with sympathy and grace. Those qualities are admired and highly valued, but they are ones that a hothouse education may fail to instil.

Chapter Four

# *Helping Young Children to Learn: Nine Practical Guidelines*

Up to now, my statements about the kinds of things that parents need to do to help children learn have been broad and rather vague. I have talked in a rather general way about making efforts to encourage children, and to provide opportunities for them and give them needed tuition, but I have said very little concerning the actual ways in which parents might achieve these ends.

The time has come to be more specific. In contrast with the earlier chapters, the present one and the two that follow are much more down-to-earth. They give practical advice for parents. This chapter concentrates on broad principles. The following ones include descriptions of a number of useful learning games and activities that parents can introduce. Although there is no intention to provide a detailed 'How To . . .' manual, I do describe a number of procedures that parents can use for helping children to gain basic skills. At the end of each chapter there is some information concerning sources of more detailed practical advice about teaching young children.

Here are the guidelines. Some of them may strike you as being largely common-sense, but others will not.

## 1 EVERY CHILD IS DIFFERENT

Above all, never forget that each child is an individual. Fortunately, parents are ideally qualified to take account of this. No one has a better understanding of a young person's unique personality and temperament, and likes and dislikes, than the child's own mother and father.

There are parents who make statements like 'Freddie won't do well at school: he's too impulsive', or 'Freddie's not too bright when it comes to school learning: Jane's the clever one in the family', as if that were the end of the matter. A wiser adult would see the situation differently, and concentrate on specifying the (learnable) skills and habits that the child still needs to learn. A more realistic and far more helpful comment about Freddie might be: 'Freddie tends to act impulsively. To make him better prepared for tasks he'll encounter at school we will play some learning games that will help him to gain the habit of carefully attending to information, and thinking before he acts.'

If a child is impulsive and easily distracted, the experience of playing games that aid concentration and encourage reflection will be especially valuable. They will help the child to gain thinking habits that are necessary for learning to read. The child will also need effective study habits in order to succeed at other learning activities that will be encountered at school. A child who is quiet and timid will learn useful skills from games and play activities that encourage greater assertiveness and better decision-making. A shy child may also need practice in communicating with others.

## 2  TIME AND ATTENTION ARE VITAL

Any parent who is seriously interested in a child's early education must be prepared to spend a substantial amount of time talking to, reading to, and playing with the child. High-quality interactions with adults provide necessary nourishment for intellectual development. There are some adults who complain that their children always seem to be demanding attention, but most parents recognize that healthy children really do need a great deal of adult attention. We ought to be far more concerned about those rare children who do *not* look for the attention of their parents than we are about normal healthy children for whom adult attention provides a kind of nourishment which they enjoy and expect.

Of course, adults may be understandably put out by the irritating ways (such as whining or making loud noises) in which children sometimes express their desire for attention. But parents who suffer from this problem should be aware that the most common reason for a child to go to such lengths to gain the attention of an adult is that more acceptable behaviours have been ignored. If parents consistently act in ways that make it very clear to the child that (1) positive and sociable behaviours will reliably produce substantial amounts of the kinds of praise and attention that the child enjoys, and that (2) disruptive behaviours will not have this effect, the problem will diminish.

## 3   TALKING TO CHILDREN: ITS IMPORTANCE

Talking *to* a child is not the same as talking *at* a child. Sadly, in many families the latter is far more common than the former. Early learning occurs especially readily in situations in which an adult and a child are involved together in some kind of a dialogue. At this stage, dialogues will not always take the form of verbal conversations. But, just as in a conversation between adults, each partner takes turns both at attending to the other individual and at taking a more active role in communicating or initiating contact. It is not a one-way process, and a conversation-like flow is maintained by both partners. Because the parent knows the child well as an individual, and is highly sensitive to the child's needs and attuned to the signals (including non-verbal ones) conveyed by the child, such dialogues provide ideal contexts for learning. In Chapter 5 I include some practical examples of effective and less effective parent–child dialogues.

## 4   TALKING TO CHILDREN: PRACTICAL GAMES

Even parents who accept the principle that talk between parent and child is a vital ingredient of early education may find it quite difficult to put their intentions into practice. The other day I spent some time at a barbecue attended by several young children and about a dozen adults. It was noticeable that, while most of the adults seemed to like the children, were attentive to them and found them interesting, none actually spoke more than a word or two to any of them. It was as if these adults did not really know how to do so. Talking to young children is not something everyone finds easy. As Allyssa McCabe (1987) points out in her excellent book *Language Games to Play with Your Child*, talking to babies and young children is rather like dancing: a few people are naturally graceful at it, but most of us are awkward and clumsy. Fortunately it is a skill that can be acquired.

McCabe uses the word 'game' in a somewhat broad sense: for her it designates a wide variety of situations in which there is pleasurable interaction between two (or more) people, usually with some kind of aim or goal in mind. By this broad definition, a large proportion of the teaching situations in which adults succeed in encouraging children to learn can be called games. Many of the most effective practical devices for encouraging young children to gain new skills undoubt-edly have a playful element. Children learn best when they are involved in activities that engage their full attention.

Here is one language game that may already be familiar. McCabe recommends it for playing with children aged between 18 months and 2 years. It is aimed at making it fun to learn how to follow directions. The game has the advantage of being suitable for use in the kinds of confined space where children tend to feel bored, such as a doctor's waiting room.

Essentially, the adult simply gives the child a series of directions, and the child tries to follow them. For instance, at first the adult might say 'Clap your hands'. After giving several different directions, one at a time, the adult might move on to giving two directions at a time, such as 'Touch your mouth then stick out your tongue', or three directions if the child seems capable of following them, or even more. In one version the child can follow each direction as the adult says it. Alternatively, the child might be told to wait until all the directions have been completed. Increasing the number of directions will help to hold the child's attention.

For a change, the child can give the directions. If there is enough space, the directions can involve going to imaginary locations. For instance, McCabe invented directions for her daughter to go to an imaginary zoo, as follows: 'Go around the sandbox three times, go straight ahead to the end of the pavement, and turn left'. She mentions that this game led to her daughter asking directions to real places such as a local shop or her grandmother's house, and even to simple map-drawing activities.

It is easy to see that even a familiar game like this one has some valuable features. On the one hand it is structured: for the child there is some point to it. On the other hand, because the game can readily be changed and modified by the adult, it is not at all difficult to adjust the level of complexity to match the child's abilities. And it is easy and natural to add elements that introduce new concepts or skills that a parent might want a child to learn, such as 'left' and 'right', for instance, or the early stages of map-making.

## 5  THE NEED FOR INFORMAL LEARNING

McCabe is by no means the only expert on early child learning who recommends that most parental teaching should take the form of games that parent and child can play together. In fact, the majority of the procedures I shall describe in the following two chapters can be regarded as being games of one kind or another. Games that a child enjoys make learning enjoyable.

Only rarely is teaching that is at all 'formal' appropriate for young children. Young children learn from whatever they are attending to, and they attend to whatever they find interesting. If previous learning experiences have been positive and happy, a child will be keen to learn more. A child will soon begin to feel discouraged if placed in learning situations in which he or she is conscious of failing to achieve what an adult expects, or if it is clear that the adult is displeased. And if the child does not want to learn what the adult wishes to teach, either there will be a fruitless battle of wits between them or the child will be unenthusiastic to learn and less than attentive.

One advantage of game situations is that they make it possible for experiences to be repeated without the child becoming bored. A substantial amount of repetition and practice is necessary when certain skills are being acquired – reading, for example – and games make it possible for the necessary repetition to be achieved in circumstances which the young child positively enjoys.

## 6  EXPLAINING TO CHILDREN

Adults must always be prepared to explain things to children and answer their questions. There is no denying that it can be irritating to have to listen to the hundredth 'Why . . .?' in a single morning. But the majority of children's questions spring from a genuine curiosity about the world and a desire to understand it better. We all like to understand the reasons for the events we witness. We also like to have unfamiliar things explained to us: in that respect children are no different from adults.

When asked (for instance) why the child is being required to abandon an enjoyable activity, it is sometimes tempting to respond by saying 'Because I say so'. It would take a superhuman adult to have a rational answer for every single question that an energetic child can pitch, but parents who are too inclined to fall back on the 'because I say so' kind of response might pause to ask themselves whether *they* would like to be treated in the same way.

Like adults, children like to be given advance warning of events, and find it much easier to cope with new situations when they are prepared for them. So young children respond much better to being told 'In five minutes we are going to have to get your coat on and go to the shop' than to 'Stop what you are doing *now*, and put your toys away'. Especially when events are potentially frightening or alarming, children (like adults) respond better if they have been told what to expect (for example, 'This afternoon we'll go and see the nurse. She will be wearing a white coat, and she'll probably ask you to . . .').

Children are not always very effective at phrasing their questions.

Sometimes their language skills let them down. On occasions a child does not fully understand what it is he or she wants to know. So parents have to make a real effort to see things from the child's perspective. Quite often, the best way to help a child understand something is to reply to a question with another question. Children may need to be helped to learn how to think things out for themselves.

## 7 STIMULATION IS NOT ENOUGH

It is not uncommon for adults to believe that all that needs to be done to help children learn is to make their environments as 'stimulating' as possible. But this is never sufficient. However stimulating the environment is, a child needs a great deal of guidance in order to learn from it. Adults are needed to interpret the external world to the child, to point out interesting things, to draw attention to what is important, and to give feedback for the child's efforts to understand.

As a demonstration of the enormous power of adult explanations to help children understand their world, the Israeli psychologist Reuven Feuerstein invites his readers to compare two simple instructions, each of which might be given by a mother to her young child:

1 Please buy three bottles of milk.
2 Please buy three bottles of milk so that we will have enough left over for tomorrow when the shops are closed.

(Feuerstein, 1980, p. 20)

Feuerstein points out that the child who complies with the first request will be simply obeying a command. With the second, by contrast, the child is also being encouraged to become involved in the reasoning that lies behind the request. The child is receiving an opportunity to anticipate events that will take place in the future, and being encouraged to think about making plans that are based on such anticipations.

Effective parents do far more to help their children learn than merely stimulating them. Throughout the world, parents spend a great deal of time in various activities that have the effect of passing on to the child a knowledge of the culture into which he or she was born. The adult who frequently interacts with a child acts as a kind of guide and interpreter to the child's environment. The child needs the parent to direct attention to what is most significant, to demonstrate how to 'read' the physical environment, and how to use it effectively. For instance, the parent can get the child to look at what is especially significant and help the child to perceive relationships between events, to make comparisons, to become aware of differences and similarities, to retain information in memory. And by encouraging the child to think about events in memory as well as objects that are physically present, the parent assists the child to become more reflective, and capable of thinking and making plans.

It is often important to be able to delay responding to events until one has had time to think. But a child has to learn to delay. That ability will not be learned in the absence of appropriate opportunities. A parent provides these, for instance, by getting a child to respond to questions like 'What do you think will happen next?' Children's imaginative powers, as well as their awareness of time in the past and in the future, can be encouraged to develop through questions such as 'What do you remember?' or 'Are you looking forward to . . .?'

## 8  PREPARING THE CHILD FOR SCHOOL

One benefit of early learning experiences is that they prepare the child to take full advantage of the opportunities that will become available when formal schooling begins. Here are two examples illustrating that important fact.

*LISTENING SKILLS AND READING*

A very common reason for children failing to make good progress at school is the lack of certain very basic skills that are needed to cope with school tasks. Accelerated learning aside, the chances of a school-child making even normal progress towards learning to read will be impeded if certain listening skills have not been gained before the beginning of formal instruction.

For instance, many schoolchildren have difficulties with learning to read because they fail to perceive the smallest sound units of language, *phonemes*. It is virtually impossible to learn to read if you cannot perceive language sounds accurately or discriminate between two different phonemes, such as the *b* in *bad* and the *d* in *dad* (Coles, 1987). One research team (Bradley and Bryant, 1983) asked 4- and 5-year-olds to listen to lists containing three words, in which every word but one contained a common phoneme (for example, *dig, dot, bun*). The child's task was to say which was the odd word. The researchers discovered that the children's performance level at this task was a good predictor of the same children's achievements at reading and spelling four years later, when they were attending school. Interestingly, there is an identical relationship between phonemic discrimination skills and progress at Braille reading in blind people. In one study it was found that all those participants who did well at a test measuring the ability to discriminate and combine phonemes did better at reading than people who failed the test. All of the latter made slower than average progress at Braille reading.

These findings establish that there is a connection between phonological skills in early childhood and subsequent progress at learning to read. Does this mean that differences in early phonological skills are a major cause of variability in children's later reading achievements? To answer that question, Bradley and Bryant next selected 65 young children who did poorly at the phoneme-discrimination task, and who therefore seemed to be 'at risk' so far as later success at reading was concerned. Some of these children were given special training, aimed mainly at helping them to learn to discriminate between simple sounds. The training was not particularly time-consuming or intensive: each child was seen for twenty ten-minute sessions per year, for two years.

The children were tested again when they were 8 years old. By this time those who had not been given any special training were lagging a year behind the normal standard of achievement at reading. Their progress at spelling was even worse: by 8 years of age they were already two whole years behind the average. By contrast, those children who had been trained to discriminate between phonemes and to make associations between sounds and letters were successfully reading at the level expected for children of their age.

So a tiny amount of time spent on making sure that young children gained simple but crucial listening skills had a huge pay-off in future years. It was enough to protect the children from experiencing serious reading difficulties when they went to school. Generally speaking, any preschool experiences that help a young child to gain basic skills involving letters, sounds, and phonemes will make it easier for the child to make steady progress in reading at school. Such experiences greatly reduce the likelihood of severe difficulties in learning to read.

A lack of fundamental skills is a common cause of failure at school tasks. For instance, it is often the true cause of the kinds of reading problem that lead to a child being diagnosed as having 'learning disabilities' or as being 'reading-disabled' or 'dyslexic'. Teachers sometimes fail to perceive that a child lacks basic skills that the ability to read depends on.

There is no need for parents to give formal training in phonological skills. When parents regularly read to their children, and encourage them to enjoy the rhyming games and other language experiences that are commonplace in homes in which books and other written materials are regularly enjoyed, the children will gain the required fundamental skills without any specific instruction. Some games that can help to promote a child's acquisition of phonological skills are described in Chapter 6.

*REHEARSING, REMEMBERING, AND LEARNING*
Another, very different, example of a fundamental skill which parents can teach to a young child without great difficulty, and which can greatly assist the child to profit from school experiences, is the ability to rehearse items that need to be remembered. It is not at all difficult to learn. Any child whose home background provides opportunities for playing language games such as the ones described in this chapter will easily gain the habit of rehearsing words whenever the demands of a task make it helpful to do so.

But compare that child with one whose language experiences at home are very limited. This child may begin school without knowing how to rehearse, and spend several years at school without learning to do so. Teachers may fail to give instruction in this skill, perhaps wrongly assuming that all children learn to rehearse before they go to school. So some individuals will spend their earliest school years lacking an ability that is essential if a young person is to get the maximum benefit from classroom instruction. They will be at a real disadvantage compared with children who have gained the habit of rehearsing.

Research studies have demonstrated that, although older school-children are more likely to rehearse than younger children when they are trying to remember information, even by the age of 10 many children do not spontaneously rehearse. Not surprisingly, those children who do rehearse remember information better than those who do not. Yet those children who do not rehearse can easily be taught to do so. (Simply telling children to whisper the names of items they are looking at until they are told to begin recalling them may be sufficient: most children find it easy to follow this instruction.) As a result, their performance at memory tasks improves dramatically. But it is not so easy to remedy the cumulative effects of failing to learn in previous years as a consequence of not rehearsing in the many different circumstances where it would have been useful for them to do so.

## 9  LEARNING MAY TAKE TIME

Finally, we should all come to terms with the fact that there are no magic short cuts to learning, either for children or for adults. People are always claiming to have invented special gimmicks that make learning much easier, or much faster. Although certain special techniques do have their uses (for instance, there are methods that are useful for some aspects of second-language learning, and mnemonic techniques that can help a person to remember new information), learning always takes time, and patience, and close attention, on the part of learner and teacher alike.

Even when a particular skill (rehearsing, for example) may be gained in a short time, it often takes much longer to acquire the *habit* of regularly and spontaneously making use of that skill in all the circumstances where it can be valuable. Only when skills are firmly established can children (or adults, for that matter) start to use them in situations and contexts that are very different from the ones in which the skills were originally acquired, or modify an existing skill in order to meet the demands of a new task.

Children sometimes gain new abilities surprisingly quickly, but we ought not to be too surprised when that does not happen. As parent teachers, you will need lots of patience, and then some more. Also, be sensitive to your child's mood. Sometimes the child will be too tired to enjoy the game you have prepared, or too fractious, or he or she may get bored with it, perhaps because of other immediate preoccupations. At those times, always be prepared to stop what you are doing and come back to it later. Children learn best when they are giving something their full attention. That doesn't often happen unless they are thoroughly enjoying what they are doing.

### FURTHER READING

Einon, Dorothy. *Creative Play*. Harmondsworth: Penguin Books, 1985.
  Describes numerous learning games for children of various ages. The games are age-graded (from birth to 10 years) and clearly illustrated, and their purposes explained. There is a list of twenty favoured toys.

Chapter Five

# *Helping Children With Language*

In Chapter 2 we discovered that it definitely is possible to accelerate a child's language development. When this happens, a child's capacities to think and to understand are also extended. So it makes a great deal of sense for parents to put some effort into nurturing their children's language. We also discovered that increasing the rate of progress does not require Herculean efforts or extraordinary dedication. Nor does it demand technical expertise or teaching skills that are beyond the reach of most parents. The most important thing to know is that children thrive on talk and other language activities.

How is faster language acquisition achieved? Essentially, all it takes is, first, an awareness of the fact that children make considerably faster progress as language users when their parents talk to them frequently and play with them at language games and other everyday activities, and, second, a willingness to spend a reasonable amount of time every day (totalling at least an hour per day, on average, if that is possible) with the child, interacting on a one-to-one basis or as near to that as circumstances permit.

As we saw in Chapter 2, those experimental interventions that have been especially successful at increasing young children's competence in language have been ones in which the parents were instructed to spend more time on language-related activities than they would otherwise have done. The parents were given advice about effective language games and practices, based on the findings of research that has investigated the causes of language development. In the present chapter I shall describe some procedures that any parent can depend on, and show how they can be put into practice.

# STARTING EARLY

Steps to encourage language acquisition can begin early in the child's first year. Although most babies do not start to say actual words until considerably later, it would be quite wrong to assume that parents should delay attending to their children's language skills until then. Encouragement needs to begin some considerable time before babies utter their 'first words', because, despite appearances, these do not represent the beginnings of language development. On the contrary, they are the *culmination* of many important changes that have already taken place over the preceding months. Consequently, the first steps to stimulate a child's language development should be taken before a baby is 6 months of age. A baby's early language experiences will accelerate vital developments that prepare the child for talking.

Starting early was a key element of the highly successful language-acceleration programme of William Fowler and his colleagues which was mentioned in Chapter 2. Almost certainly, the fact that the parents were taught to pay attention to language skills at an earlier-than-usual stage in their babies' lives was a major reason for their children rapidly gaining several months in their ability to talk.

What are the practical steps that a parent should take to stimulate language development in the early months? Precisely what can a parent do? To start with, it is helpful to keep in mind that a number of a baby's activities will have communicative functions well before the talking stage. Crying and smiling, for example, and sucking, cooing, and gurgling as well, are all ways of telling people about needs and feelings. Research has shown that mothers who make sensitive efforts to 'read' these messages help the baby to progress towards mastering increasingly sophisticated ways of communicating, culminating with spoken language. One researcher, Mary Ainsworth, established that babies whose mothers attend promptly to their young infant's cries, and do what they can to soothe them, tend to make faster-than-average progress towards mastering more advanced communicative skills, including language. The more sensitively the mother responds to the baby's signals, the more speedy is the baby's progress as a communicator (Ainsworth *et al.*, 1974).

Talking and singing are two of the most effective ways to soothe a young baby. They are also good ways to encourage the baby to smile. And when an infant starts to coo, this also can be encouraged by talk and by body language which tells the child that these prelinguistic communications are being enjoyed. One very simple game that parents can play with their infant involves the parent just waiting for the child to coo, and then, from a position of about one foot away, paying full attention to the baby and talking back in a high-pitched voice, as well as giving any other responses (such as kisses and hugs) that the parent cares to add. After a few tries at this exercise, baby and parent will be able to build up to a sequence of turn-taking. Allyssa McCabe, who recommends this game, points out that since you are more skilled in responding appropriately to your child than he or she is to you, it is a good idea to let the baby initiate the game.

At around this stage, real language games can be effective. Songs and lullabies such as 'Rock-a-bye-Baby' and 'Brahms' Lullaby' may already have proved their worth for soothing the infant. Babies will also enjoy other songs, including 'Twinkle, Twinkle, Little Star' and 'Three Blind Mice'. A mother or father can act these out, as well as songs which the parent has invented.

There is no need to be too concerned about the fact that a baby cannot fully 'understand' songs at this stage. This does not mean that the songs will not contribute to a child's language development. The child will be becoming familiar with the sounds and the rhythms of language, and starting to learn to attend to and 'tune in' to social communications.

At some point, with songs that are also language games, such as 'Pat-a-Cake, Pat-a-Cake', 'Peek-a-Boo', or 'Ride a Cock Horse', the child will gradually start to play a more active part. The child will take turns with the parent, learning how to alternate between active and attentive roles, and thereby gaining some of the skills that make it possible to enjoy a dialogue or a conversation.

It may be a long time before the child actively imitates the parent's actions – possibly not until the age of 7 or 8 months – but well before this time the child will be enjoying the sounds, learning that certain familiar actions are signalled by words, and learning to anticipate action routines on hearing the appropriate language messages. A good way to encourage a child to make physical gestures in response to your language messages is to give repeated performances of a few very simple gestures (such as waving 'bye-bye'), and at the same time say aloud the appropriate words.

All these experiences contribute to the gradual acquisition of communicative skills. Sooner or later, the child will gain the amazing capacity (one that is unparalleled by even the most powerful computers) of being able to make sense of the patterns of sounds that we humans identify as the flow of language.

## BABY TALK

Twenty years ago, when my children were toddlers, parents were strongly advised to avoid baby talk at all costs. We were told that it would confuse babies and impede their language development. Experts warned that baby talk would simply encourage toddlers to learn words that would later have to be unlearned. Today's experts have a more relaxed attitude. They agree that baby talk is technically incorrect and ungrammatical, but they also point out that it not only gives pleasure to babies and adults alike, but has genuine communicative functions. The mother who talks to her baby is not simply engaged in teaching grammatically correct language. As Harvey Wiener points out in *Talk With Your Child* (1988), talk is a social tool that we use to help us understand one another. Baby talk can be a means by which the sensitive parent is able to tune into the child's thoughts.

For these reasons, there is more to be lost than to be gained from always trying to talk to a child in precisely the same way as you would talk to an adult. In order to improve communication with a young child, and to help both of the partners in a dialogue to focus on the same thoughts and meanings, it is often sensible for parents to abandon some of the rules of adult language. For a baby who has only just begun the lengthy process of mastering language, the kinds of utterance that communicate most effectively will often be very different from the forms of communication that mature language users might prefer. It is worth remembering that language is a tool for communication, not an end in itself.

To master language, a child has to gain many skills that involve perceiving and producing *sounds*, and also many skills that are related to understanding *meanings*. Sometimes it can be helpful to make things simpler for the child by keeping these two elements separate. So even those sounds that go beyond baby talk in the extent to which they are nonsensical or without meaning can have a place in language development. A good language game that parents can play to encourage babies aged 6 months or more to attend to the sounds and rhythms of language, and to imitate them as well, involves the adult repeatedly saying nonsense syllables ('blup', 'boop', 'dub', for instance). The child is at first rewarded for responding with any sounds at all. Gradually, the responses become increasingly accurate imitations of the syllable uttered by the adult.

# ENCOURAGING EARLY LANGUAGE: TWELVE PRACTICAL STEPS

Here are some additional practical steps that parents can take to communicate more effectively with babies and children, and nurture the growth of early language. In each case, the advice is soundly based on the findings of research into children's language development.

## 1  PITCH YOUR VOICE HIGH

Young children are especially sensitive to high-pitched sounds. They tend not to respond to the lower-pitched sounds that adults generally use. So, in order to gain a baby's attention, you should be prepared to raise the pitch of your voice. Of course, high-pitched speech is easier for women than for men, and adults may understandably feel that there is something undignified about the whole idea. But give it a try, anyway, even if at first you feel it necessary to take the precaution of doing it when no other grown-ups are around. Your child's smiles will be an ample reward.

## 2  VARY YOUR VOICE

When talking to a young child you should put more variation into your voice than when speaking to an adult. As well as concentrating on the higher pitches, use a wider range of pitch than you would in adult talk. Accent particular words, or parts of words, that you want to emphasize. Exaggerate words, and be prepared to repeat them. Use more facial expressions than you normally would, and accompany your words with physical actions. Don't hesitate to use 'silly' ones, such as sticking out your tongue.

The reason for adding all these non-linguistic elements is that, because the child's language skills are so rudimentary, in order to understand you he or she needs all the extra help that is available. The meaning of a message will be clearer to a child if the language is accompanied by appropriate actions. Games in which words are combined with actions (for example, '*Up* you go and *down* you go', 'Here comes the kissing monster', 'I'm going to tickle you', all acted out appropriately) will help to get a verbal message across.

Also, place more emphasis on intonation that you would when talking to an adult. A rising voice and other special intonations can give extra clues to the child. They can help to engage the child's attention and show when a response is required. Because the baby's language competence is incomplete, be prepared to introduce any extra cues you can think of to aid communication. These additional cues can be both verbal and non-verbal. As well as reducing the extent to which the child's understanding of what you are expressing depends on every word being correctly processed, extra cues can help to attract the baby's attention and maintain his or her concentration on what you are saying.

## 3 PLAY VOCABULARY GAMES

There are a number of games that will help to increase the child's vocabulary. In the early months a fair amount of patience will be required, as words will need to be repeated many times. McCabe recommends some activities that will encourage a baby to hook up early sounds to meanings. For instance, the parent draws attention to something and keeps naming it while talking about it ('Here's *Teddy*, what a nice *Teddy*, can you stroke *Teddy*?'). Or the parent points to a number of instances of the same thing ('Here's a car, and there's a car, and here's another car'). As the child begins to make obvious progress, the vocabulary games can become more sophisticated. Simply naming things and then talking about them will help your child to gain a larger vocabulary. In another game the parent draws attention to features which parent and child share. For instance, 'There's Mummy's eyes, Bobby's eyes. Here's Mummy's nose. Where's Bobby's nose? Where's Mummy's mouth?'

## 4 KEEP LANGUAGE SIMPLE

Keep sentences simple and short. Be prepared to repeat unfamiliar sentences. Like adults, babies and young children who do not understand something on the first presentation often comprehend better when what is being said is more familiar.

## 5 WHISPER

It is often a good idea to whisper. This can help the child to gain the habit of carefully attending to another person, and 'tuning in' to what they are saying. Toddlers enjoy it when adults whisper to them, and they like to whisper themselves. For young children whispering is yet another educational language game. It also extends their knowledge about the range of different ways in which language can be used.

6  SPEAK SLOWLY

Any new and unfamiliar language (and that includes one's own first language) is even more confusing to young children than it is to adults. By speaking fairly slowly an adult can make the task of comprehending language easier.

7  GIVE A CHILD TIME TO RESPOND

It is important to give your child opportunities to respond to what you say. You must be prepared to wait for this to happen. Many adults have a tendency to get anxious if a child does not react immediately, and quickly rush in to 'fill the void'. Try not to do this, because it may prevent a child from making an utterance he or she was getting ready to make. If a reaction does not come very quickly, just relax and wait for a few seconds before continuing. Research by Paula Menyuk (1977) has shown that infants who develop effective communication skills usually have parents who do not just talk at them but are careful to give them time to talk, and are also careful to respond to their signals.

8  USE RHYME AND RHYTHM

Introduce rhyme and rhythm into your language. Rhymes, songs, and rhyming games are all enjoyed by young children. Even in later childhood, many of the playground games to which children are naturally drawn are ones that have these elements. Other things apart, they aid a child who is learning to use language by making its structure easier to discern. As you will have noticed when you listen to an unfamiliar foreign language, even basic information, such as where words begin and end, is often hidden from the novice. Rhythm can help by giving extra clues that help a child perceive the underlying word structure. Rhythms also seem to provide a way of coordinating language production with body movements. They often soothe or calm a young child.

An advantage of rhyming words is that they provide opportunities for children to enjoy the *sounds* of language. Most parents and children enjoy nursery rhymes. Don't be too quick to dismiss them as being too old-fashioned or not relevant to today's world. Much of their value for young children comes from the opportunities they provide for becoming comfortable and familiar with language and its rhymes and rhythms. Rhymes can also help a child discover how to understand a simple narrative.

Don't hesitate to make up rhymes yourself, preferably ones that incorporate the child's name, or the names of familiar objects or people.

## 9 SPEAK DIRECTLY TO THE CHILD

Research findings demonstrate that a particularly important principle – perhaps the most crucial of all – is to make sure that the language stimulation a child receives is as *direct* as possible.

Direct language stimulation involves language specifically targeted at the child. This can be observed in any interchange or conversation in which an adult and child take turns. It is the language of someone who is talking *with* the child, and who is sensitive to the child's needs and state of mind. It contrasts with the language behaviour of, say, a mother who talks a great deal in a child's presence but without specifically talking with or to the child or being much aware of the child's presence.

As we have seen, babies' language development is not helped by parents who just talk steadily at the child, without providing opportunities for participation. So far as language acquisition is concerned, research findings have shown that the sheer amount of language to which children are exposed is, perhaps surprisingly, not important at all. But the quantity of *direct* language they encounter has a strong influence on the rate at which they gain language skills. So talk to your child as often as you can. As we saw in Chapter 2, children make fast progress when adults talk to them regularly and frequently, and engage them in conversational dialogues.

## 10 MATCH YOUR TALK TO THE CHILD'S MENTAL ACTIVITY

Research has shown that it is particularly valuable for adults to talk to babies about things they are already looking at. This is not always easy, of course: it may require a good deal of sensitivity on the part of the adult. But when the adult can succeed in discovering what items or events are currently engaging a child's attention, and then speaks to the child about them, the language input is likely to be highly beneficial.

Young children, until they are around 2 years of age, find it much easier to think about things they can actually see. So if an adult is talking about something that is physically present, and already engaging the child's attention, the likelihood of an exact match between the adult's language and the child's thinking is greatly increased. Talking about something the child is already attending to is a powerful way to tune in to the child's thinking.

There are a number of practical steps that will increase the likelihood of a good match between the adult's language and the child's current thoughts. For example, when a baby is engaged with pictures or toys it is generally easier for the adult to know precisely what is being attended to than at a moment when the baby is just sitting and looking around. So it might be helpful for an adult to start a conversation by talking about, say, an animal depicted in a book that the child is looking at. A nice example of this appears in the following mother–child dialogue. They are looking at a picture book.

*Mother*: What's the little boy doing?
*Child*: Ladder
*Mother*: Climbing up a ladder. What's he getting on to, on the roof isn't he? Who's up there Rosemary? Who's that?
*Child*: Pussycat
*Mother*: Ye . . . es. What's the pussycat doing do you think?
*Child*: Jump out
*Mother*: Jump out do you think? Can she jump out? Think the little boy will catch her?
*Child*: Yes
(Quoted by Czerniewska, 1985, from *Baby Talk*, BBC Radio 4, 1982)

Notice that the adult is not some kind of 'supermum': she is just doing what many mothers regularly do. All the same, she is doing a superb teaching job by helping her child to think, and talk, about the events shown in the picture book. She starts by getting the child to think about the actions being performed by the little boy in the picture. When the child replies 'Ladder', she interprets and expands on this terse statement, then encourages the child to think about the little boy's reason for climbing the ladder, and the purpose he has in mind. The child is being given an opportunity to understand things from another person's (the little boy's) perspective, and understand something of that person's state of mind. (This kind of understanding is basic to mature human social bahaviour: autistic people, who lack the ability to think in this way, are consequently unable to function independently.) When the mother switches attention to the pussycat and asks the child to anticipate what will happen next, she is providing an opportunity for the child to practise reflective thinking.

## 11  ASK QUESTIONS THAT ENCOURAGE THINKING

A parent's questions are an extremely important means of stretching a child's linguistic skills. Contrast the above conversation with the following, imaginary one, and notice how, on this occasion, the parent fails to give the child the same kinds of opportunity:

*Father*: There's a little boy. What colour is his shirt?
*Child*: Red
*Father*: Yes, and what is he climbing on?
*Child*: Ladder
*Father*: What's at the top of the ladder?
*Child*: Pussycat
*Father*: That's right. Is it a big pussycat or a little pussycat?

So far as the child's learning is concerned, there is a world of difference between the first conversation and the second. The father in the second dialogue is, like the mother in the first, patiently reading to the child, directing the child's attention to important things in the picture, responding to the child's statements, and maintaining some kind of a conversation. However, it is all too easy to see that he is not doing anything like so good a job as an educator. The child is not being encouraged to think about the actions of the participants, or to anticipate what is going to happen next, or to see things from the perspective of the actors depicted in the picture. The parent is not drawing language out in the way that happened in the previous dialogue.

Essentially, where the father is failing is in not asking questions that really stretch the child's capacity to think and communicate. This is another enormously important aspect of parents' teaching activities. Cast your mind back to the experiment by Whitehurst *et al.* which I described in Chapter 2. You may recall that in that study some middle-class parents, all of whom regularly read to their children even before the project began, were simply taught better ways of talking to their children when they were reading to them from picture books. The instructions to parents were simple: for instance, they were told to ask 'What?' questions – designed to help a child participate more actively in the story-telling – and to encourage children to talk about the contents of the pictures. In other words, the brief training (lasting just one hour) was designed to encourage the parents to do exactly the kinds of things that the mother was doing in the first of the two conversations above and that the father in the second (fictional) conversation failed to do. And as we saw, the training had very dramatic positive effects. After just one month, the children of the trained parents were at least six months ahead of children in a control group whose parents read to them just as often. The benefits were also long-lasting: they were maintained for at least nine months after the study began.

What kinds of questions are best? Essentially, ones that stimulate language and thought. In practice, these are often ones that begin with 'Why?', 'What?', or 'How?' Generally speaking, such questions encourage the child to answer in the child's own terms, and say what he or she thinks is happening. So, when the mother asked her child 'What's the pussycat doing?', she was encouraged to think about what was going on in the picture.

Young children do not always fully understand what is being asked by a 'Why?' question, but that does not matter too much so long as they realize that they are being required to think. To use Harvey Wiener's words, good questions succeed in stimulating a child's communicative skills because they 'invite the participation of a mind stimulated by challenge' (Wiener, 1988, p. 59). Wiener points out that a child's participation is clearly stimulated by questions such as 'Why did the spider frighten Miss Muffett away?', or 'What do you think we should tell Daddy about our afternoon in the park?', or 'How are you going to make your pretend cookies?' The child's participation is less likely to be stimulated by questions such as 'Do you like Miss Muffett?', or 'Did you enjoy your afternoon in the park?' Wiener suggests that parents would be wise to avoid questions that require only 'yes' or 'no' responses. They tend to slam the door on real conversation, and therefore make no real contribution to language development.

That does not mean that parents should never ask about the names of objects or never ask specific, 'closed' questions, that require a particular answer. In fact, the mother in our earlier dialogue did include a number of such direct requests for specific information. She asked, for instance, 'Who's up there Rosemary?' On one occasion she even included a yes–no question ('Think the little boy will catch her?').

There is no one particular type of question that is always going to be appropriate. The purpose of asking questions is to encourage children to expand their thoughts and communications, and to participate more and more. Within a conversation between parent and child any question, whatever form it takes, is a good one if it helps to achieve this.

## 12  DON'T BE TOO CONCERNED ABOUT A CHILD'S MISTAKES

Don't be too anxious to correct errors in a young child's language. As was shown in one of the studies described in Chapter 2, excessive parental concern with correct pronunciation can actually impede a child's progress. It is sometimes useful to expand the child's sentences into fuller and more conventional forms, but the reason for doing this is simply to help the child communicate better.

## ENCOURAGING LANGUAGE AS THE CHILD GETS OLDER

Many parents take great pride and delight in their child's language progress in the earliest years, but pay less and less attention to language skills as the child gets older. Harvey Wiener points out that in many homes the amount of actual conversation between parent and child is remarkably small (Wiener, 1988). There are a number of reasons for this. Television is one. Parental preoccupation with other responsibilities – perhaps a new baby – is another. The tendency for younger and younger children to spend time at formal classes in such things as ballet, art, music, or gymnastics, and the increasing use of kindergarten or day-care, has had the unfortunate effect of reducing the amount of time that parents and children are together, engaged in some shared activity. Wiener argues that, although many other kinds of learning experience are valuable, the time that a child and parent spend talking together is an especially rich source of opportunities for learning.

Even when the child does spend a lot of time with other adults or is engaged in structured learning situations there may be rather few instances of the kinds of verbal interaction that stretch a child's mind. When time is passed with babysitters or other adults there is no guarantee that such opportunities will be frequent. Wiener points out that, sometimes,

> There's lots of talking *to* and *at* but little talking *with*. Do you note the engagement of ideas and their expansion through discussion, explanation, and application? Do you hear more than isolated chatter . . .? Are there verbal interactions, questions and answers, assertions and judgments, requests and related actions? To share the fabric of language and, later, the reading and writing skills inextricably woven into its development, your child needs a con-

versational partner – gentle, loving, open-minded, inquiring, respectful, patient, relaxed, intelligent. (Wiener, 1988, p. 4–5)

Wiener believes that conversation is the pathway to knowledge. He thinks that valuable opportunities to help children learn are lost when parents spend too little time conversing with their children, and suggests that all parents should take steps to establish what he terms a 'conversational family'. This can be achieved by any parents who consistently adopt most of the following rules:

▶ 1 Engage actively in play with children.
▶ 2 Ask questions often; invite question-asking.
▶ 3 Listen thoughtfully to responses; ask more questions.
▶ 4 Tell stories; read stories; act out stories; discuss stories.
▶ 5 Discuss the day's best and worst moments.
▶ 6 In facing decisions with your child, review options; then ask your child about the reasons for the final choice.
▶ 7 Whenever possible eat meals together; talk to each other at meals.
▶ 8 Shut off the car radio on a family drive.
▶ 9 Shut off the television frequently when the whole family is together.
▶10 No headphones allowed at home if someone else is present.
▶11 If it can be avoided, don't talk on the telephone if someone else is present in the room.

(Wiener, 1988, p. 34)

Wiener has also produced a 25-item 'conversational inventory', to which parents are invited to respond in order to evaluate their 'use of and attitudes towards talking with young children'. To end this chapter, I list below a few points adapted from Wiener's inventory. Together with the above rules they provide a first-rate brief guide to the kinds of conversational activity that are especially helpful to a growing child.

● First, Wiener asks whether you share *your* daily experiences in conversation with your child?

● Second, do you give your child frequent opportunities to hear you engage in discussions about events, movies you have seen, books you have read, and so on?

● Third, do you invite your child's opinions about things such as clothing, a new food, a television programme?

- Fourth, do you give children choices and encourage them to make decisions for themselves? Do you encourage them to explain why they made their choice?

- Fifth, is your child encouraged to answer the telephone? Have you taught the child how to make calls and respond to them?

- And sixth, do you encourage the child to expand on very brief replies made to questions?

## FURTHER READING

Crystal, David. *Listen to Your Child.* Harmondsworth: Penguin Books, 1986.
An interesting book for parents who would like to pay closer attention to their children's language development.
McCabe, Allyssa. *Language Games to Play with Your Child.* New York: Fawcett Columbine, 1987.
A very good source of practical language games.
Wiener, Harvey S. *Talk With Your Child.* New York: Penguin Books, 1988.
An excellent guide to all practical aspects of language acquisition. Includes a very useful section describing the author's fifty favourite books for children.

Chapter Six

# *Getting Prepared for Reading*

As with the previous chapter, the intention here is not to provide a complete account of what to teach and how to teach it, but simply to illustrate the kinds of learning games and activities that a parent can encourage a child to play.

Some children learn to read at the age of 3 or 4, with only a modest amount of help and encouragement from their parents. Most of these children will have acquired an intense interest in books at an early stage, leading to a desire to discover for themselves the exciting contents of books that are new or unfamiliar, and a strong motivation to gain the reading skills that make this possible. I hope that the parents of these children will find this chapter useful, but to be frank it has not been written primarily for them. Foremost in my mind have been the needs of children who are not quite so self-confident and independent, or so keen to read, at least in their earliest years.

## GETTING PRIORITIES RIGHT

Many parents are anxious about their young children's future progress in learning to read when they go to school. Their anxiety is not unreasonable: many children do experience difficulties. Contrary to popular opinion, in the vast majority of cases the reason is not that the child has a specific disorder or reading disability. Almost always, the real reason is that the child has failed to gain certain basic language skills that are a necessary foundation for learning to read. For instance, as we saw in Chapter 4, in order to learn to read you have to be able to discriminate between the smallest units of speech, the phonemes. Children who listen carefully to words and succeed at phoneme-discrimination tasks usually make good progress at reading. But children who lack these listening skills cannot learn to read. Those children whose parents regularly read to them will normally gain the skills without any special efforts being made. However, children whose home life does not include experiences with books and written language may fail to acquire them. If that happens they will begin school with a real disadvantage. The problems are often compounded when early failures at school make a young person anxious about reading. As a result, a child may be unable to concentrate on the kinds of learning that would help remedy the deficiences. This can make matters even worse.

As I remarked in Chapter 2, there is nothing particularly surprising or hard to explain about the failure of some children to learn to read. For a child who begins school ill-prepared for it, perhaps because the parents have not provided appropriate experiences with language and written letters and words, the experience of learning to read at school can be like a difficult obstacle course. A child who has been deprived in this way will encounter opportunities for failing at many points along the way. And even in the best of schools, a teacher who is responsible for thirty children from varying home backgrounds may fail to see that a particular child is having difficulties caused by a lack of, say, listening skills or letter-identification abilities that the majority of the children in the classroom will have acquired in the course of everyday reading activities at home. It takes years to learn to read really fluently, and a child at school who becomes aware that he or she is making slower progress than other boys and girls may easily be discouraged.

So for many parents a sensible first priority would be to make sure that the child does gain some of the very basic skills needed for reading. Understandably, many mothers and fathers would like their child to read at an early age, but it is no tragedy if this does not happen. Some children learn to read at 3 or 4, before they go to school, but others are not sufficiently prepared at that age, or just not interested in reading on their own.

If a child's home background has provided opportunities for gaining enough familiarity with spoken and written language to gain elementary skills such as the ones that make it possible to learn to identify sounds and letters, the child will learn readily enough when taught reading at school. Compared with those children who have learned to read much earlier, the child may be at a slight disadvantage; but that will be nothing compared with the child's advantages over those others who, as a result of major deficiencies in home reading and language experiences, do have serious problems. What is more, the child who is less than enthusiastic about learning to read when very young may well make faster progress at other abilities, compared with keener young readers.

So even if you would like your child to learn to read before beginning formal schooling, it might be unwise to attach too much importance to this. For many parents it is more sensible to give priority to making sure that the child is adequately *prepared* to learn, whenever the child's own needs and interests, or the expectations of schoolteachers, make this desirable. You may well find that your efforts are more successful than you intended.

## FITTING IN WITH THE SCHOOL

Some parents fear that a child who starts to learn to read before beginning school will become confused when school reading instruction begins. They may hesitate to teach their child because they fear that they will be seen as pushy parents who are simply making the teacher's job more difficult.

Thirty years ago many people thought that teaching should be left to schoolteachers. Nowadays almost everyone knows better, especially in the teaching profession. Primary teachers are sensitive to the fact that every child is unique, particularly in the extent to which experiences at home will have prepared the child for school learning.

Occasional minor clashes and slight confusions resulting from differences of approach to learning at home and at school are probably inevitable, but should not cause great concern. The problems would be most acute for a child whose teaching at home followed a rigid course of formal instruction. If, on beginning school, that child had to switch to a very different but equally tightly structured course of instruction, real problems could arise. But providing that home teaching is largely informal, not closely structured, and based largely on games and play experiences, there need be no serious difficulties. Although methods of teaching differ, the skills that a reader requires remain the same. If a child has gained such skills at home, they will contribute towards the child's progress as a reader, whatever method of instruction is being followed.

## READING TO YOUNG CHILDREN

As has been emphasized in previous chapters, sessions in which a parent reads to a child are valuable in many different ways. Language skills are extended, of course, and so are abilities to reason, to reflect, and to imagine, particularly when the parent encourages the child to participate actively by the kinds of 'What?' (as in "What do you think the little girl is going to do next?") and 'Why?' questions that were discussed in Chapter 2.

Babies can be introduced to books well before they are capable of understanding stories. Six-month-olds will enjoy looking at books based entirely on pictures. Babies are obviously attracted to pictures of animals and simple objects, and pictures of other babies are a particular source of fascination. Even when little or no language is involved, much of value will be learned.

At first the baby will not even understand that pictures represent real objects. Babies have to learn to interpret pictures. This ability depends on thinking skills that make it possible for a two-dimensional pattern of marks on paper to be viewed as denoting a three-dimensional object. This is one of many basic abilities which, because we acquired them when we were too young to remember, we tend to forget that they once had to be learned. In fact, no baby is born with the ability to recognize objects from pictures: it has to be acquired.

Apart from the chances they provide for learning about words, sounds, letters, and so on, and for extending a child's thinking skills, reading sessions in which the child is mainly the listener are the best opportunities for the child to discover that reading is fun and enjoyable, and also extremely useful. By reading regularly and often to a child, a parent is doing more than providing many opportunities for learning. The parent is also modelling one of the ways in which 'big people' like to spend their time.

## PRE-READING ACTIVITIES

Most of the language games described in Chapter 5, especially those that encourage children to be aware of words and their sounds, make valuable pre-reading activities. They can help a child to learn certain elementary facts about reading. Adults may need to be reminded that someone who is not yet literate may have only a hazy notion of what a word actually is. It is largely *because* we are able to read that the way in which language divides itself into words is so obvious to most adults. A young child will have to learn where words begin and end: this is by no means always obvious from everyday spoken language.

In Chapter 5 I drew attention to the value of games that encourage a child to become aware of rhyme and rhythm in language. These games help children to gain the basic listening skills that the young reader will need. A child who lacks such skills may find it impossible to learn to read, as was discovered in the investigation by Bradley and Bryant (1983) that was described in Chapter 4.

The youngest children will need a fair amount of assistance before they can start to enjoy the more advanced language games. In the following dialogue, in which parent and child are engaged in a game where one partner chooses a simple word and then each takes it in turn to provide a word that rhymes with it, the parent happily steps in to give help whenever it is needed:

*Child*: Car
*Mother*: Far
*Child*: I can't think of another one.
*Mother*: What do we keep our jam and marmalade in? It's made of glass and sounds like car, far.
*Child*: Oh! Jar
*Mother*: That's right. Tar
*Child*: What's that?
*Mother*. It's the black sticky stuff that workmen put on the roads.
(Baker, 1980, p. 22)

Notice also that the parent is not strictly binding herself to following the exact rules of the game. She improvises, and interrupts the game at one time, in order to supply useful information.

Other valuable pre-reading activities include games in which children learn to look carefully and concentrate on how things appear. Simple games that parent and child can play includes ones in which the child spots the differences between similar objects, or discriminates between objects on the basis of a physical dimension ('Which kitten is the bigger/fatter/taller/darker?'), or looks for the 'odd one out'. Other games can help the child learn to group objects and discriminate between them on the basis of colour.

Games that encourage children to learn about shapes and physical dimensions will enable a young person to gain basic skills that are needed by the young reader in order to identify letters and words, and tell the different letters apart. In learning to recognize shapes such as circles, triangles, squares, and rectangles, the child will master most of the different shapes that are encountered in the various letters of the alphabet. Carol Baker recommends games in which children learn about shapes such as circles by playing with them, colouring them, grading them from biggest to smallest, and identifying circles to be found in the home (in plates, lids, and wheels, for instance). Then the child can go on to play similar games with other shapes, and games that involve sorting different shapes and discriminating between them.

It is also essential for the child to have a good understanding of directions and directed movements. A reader has to know in what direction to scan the text, and what to do on reaching the end of a line. (Yet another item of knowledge that is obvious to an adult but nevertheless has to be acquired by a child.) The meanings of terms like forwards, backwards, up, down, sideways, need to be understood. One game that Baker recommends for teaching these concepts involves giving the child simple instructions to move in different directions: for example, 'Take one jump backwards. Now two hops forward. Now take two steps to the left.' Later on, to encourage a child to gain the habit of making the left-to-right eye movements that are needed in reading, the parent can draw matched objects on paper, which the child joins together by drawing a line from the object on the left (a dog, for instance) to the one on the right (a bone, perhaps).

## HOW CHILDREN LEARN TO READ

Gradually, play activities that incorporate actual reading can be introduced. Most methods of reading instruction combine two different approaches. Each of them teaches important components of reading, but is incomplete on its own. In one approach, most commonly called 'look and say' but also sometimes known as the 'whole word' or 'sight' approach, the child is encouraged to learn to identify whole words. Each word is recognized by sight, and the child learns to recognize a substantial number of words in this way. In contrast, with the 'phonic' or 'sound' approach to reading, the child learns to decode words by discovering how words are made up from smaller units. Since a word is made up of a number of separate sounds (or phonemes), a child who learns how to identify the sounds, and how sounds and letters correspond with each other, ought, in principle, to be able to read.

From an adult perspective, the phonic approach might seem to be clearly superior to the look-and-say approach. The former involves learning the rules by which language is constructed. If the child knows the rules and how to apply them, reading should be easy. Look-and-say simply involves memorizing letter combinations that form words. A child who has learned only in this way can recognize the words that have been memorized, but will have little success with unfamiliar words. Lacking the ability to decipher words, the child will need assistance whenever a new word is encountered.

In practice, although the look-and-say approach has clear limitations, it does have a useful role in the early stages of learning to read. It is valuable because it helps the beginning reader to make useful progress at a time when a child taught exclusively by a phonic approach would find it hard to get off the ground. For instance, the child can start reading with whole sentences that are meaningful and interesting. Right from the outset, reading can involve attending to the meanings of words. Typically, a book for beginning readers will combine words with pictures of the objects they represent, so the picture cues will help the child to recognize each word. In this way the child can soon build up a vocabulary of useful common words that are instantly recognized. Once this is achieved, the child will be spared the tedium of having to carefully decipher every single word.

A person who can recognize the one hundred most common words will be able to read as many as half the words in a simple passage of writing, and a knowledge of no more than twelve words will enable a quarter of words in books to be identified. So it is easy to see that a child who has managed to gain even a small reading vocabulary will have a useful head start. Such a child will be encouraged by feeling that he or she is 'already reading' at a very early stage. At the same time, those words in a passage that are familiar to a child will provide useful clues to the possible meanings of the words that are not yet familiar.

A child instructed by a solely phonic approach would have rather a tedious time at first, because reading materials would be limited to short and simple single words, *dog, dig, dug*, and so on. Also, if the child was having to concentrate on single letters it would be difficult to learn to see words as wholes. As a result, reading would be likely to be rather stilted and lacking in fluency. So, although on the whole it is true to say that phonic approaches provide a superior way to teach a child to read, look-and-say techniques can and do play a useful role, particularly in the early stages. They help a young child to gain a valuable starting vocabulary of words that can be recognized on sight. They also give a child the confidence that comes from making progress and the interest and enthusiasm that follow early successes at reading meaningful written language.

When a child moves on from pre-reading activities to reading as such, certain decisions have to be made. First, what should you call the letters that occur in reading games? Should you say their names, as in *ay bee see dee*, or is it better to say their sounds, as in *a buh cuh duh*? By and large, it is best to keep to the sounds, which are far more helpful for the beginning reader. For instance, as Carol Baker observes, with the word *dog*, spelling it out with the letter names, *dee oh jee*, does not give the child much help at all. But the sounds, *duh o guh*, will take a child a long way towards reading the word.

Second, should you emphasize capitals or lower-case letters, or both? They are surprisingly different, and for the sake of simplicity it is usually best to keep to lower-case letters at first. It is not possible to ignore capitals entirely, because some of the first words a child will become familiar with contain them. Names are normally written with capitals, for example. But when you are making materials for reading games it is generally best to include only lower-case letters. Most books for young readers follow this convention.

Cards with words and names written on them form the basis of many reading games, and help to make written words a familiar part of the child's everyday environment. But there is little point in having word cards to label objects all over the house unless there is real encouragement for the child to attend to them. At first, the child needs to learn the basic principle that words can stand for people and familiar things. Even the simplest procedures can be helpful, such as drawing the child's attention to words on packages and other items in the everyday environment. One good game for encouraging a child to recognize words involves pointing to a word that appears more than once in the same book, and getting the child to look for other instances of it. Or the same game can be played with single letters. In another game, the parent makes a shopping list, with pictures of foods on the left side and their names on the right. After carefully showing each word to the child, the parent can ask the child to 'read' the list back during the shopping expedition. Afterwards, the parent can try folding the list down the middle and asking the child to identify the words with the corresponding pictures out of sight.

You should look for occasions when it is fun for the child to practise using the words that can already be recognized. For example, when the table is laid, a child will enjoy putting name cards at each person's place. When you are preparing food, the child might enjoy putting an appropriate word card on each item of food, or placing a card on each garment in a pile of clothing. Or shuffle a pack of cards with the names of the main furnishings and objects in the room, and ask the child to walk round and place each card in the appropriate place. It will often be useful to start with cards that contain both a word and a picture. The picture can be folded back when it is not longer needed. As soon as the child can recognize a few separate words on cards, he or she can be encouraged to make up stories by combining words together. It is useful to make sure that you have a good supply of materials such as white and coloured cards, glue, scissors, pens or crayons, gummed paper, and paper shapes. Carol Baker recommends that you keep a notebook containing a record of all the words your child learns. In the early stages you will need to prepare a substantial number of word cards, and it is sensible to aim at some uniformity in their size and format.

Detailed advice about the nuts and bolts of teaching your child to read is readily available. I particularly recommend Carol Baker's *Reading Through Play*. Another interesting book, though not quite so down-to-earth as Baker's, is *Teach Your Child to Read*, by Peter Young and Colin Tyre. It describes approaches such as 'paired reading' and 'shared reading' which have prove effective for helping children who have been experiencing difficulties. The essence of these methods is that adult and child read *together*, side by side. With the very young reader, they have the advantage of making it possible for a child to participate and learn in sessions that start with the parent doing most of the active reading, preferably from a book that is already familiar to the child.

Paired and shared reading approaches avoid the necessity to keep a clear distinction between books which the parent reads and the child listens to and enjoys, and 'reading books' which are carefully designed, from a limited vocabulary of short words, to match the limited skills of the early reader, but which are not always as interesting or imaginative as other books. These approaches make it possible for a child's favourite 'listening' books to contribute to the development of reading skills. Sometimes the child can simply keep up with the text, with the aid of a parental finger, or the child's own. At other times the parent may stop and ask what comes next, or ask some other question about the story. Or the adult can introduce 'finding' games: for instance, 'Where's the letter *b*?', 'Which are the big letters?', 'How many words begin with *l*?', 'See how many *t*s you can find', 'Where's a word that ends in *d*?' At a later stage, the parent can still play 'Where?' (or 'I spy . . .') games, but add more difficult ones, games that encourage the child to develop advanced reading skills. Examples are: 'Where is a word that rhymes with . . .?', 'Find me the syllable *ing*', 'I spy a word that means the opposite of . . .', 'Find me a word that means the same as . . .'. Whenever the child gets tired or restless, or does not seem to be enjoying the games, the parent can revert to taking the more active role.

## THE VITAL ROLE OF MOTIVATION

I have already said that parents' efforts to get a child involved in learning games and activities will succeed only if the child genuinely enjoys those activities, and this point cannot be over-emphasized. There will be many occasions on which a child wants to play a game, but there will be other times when the child is less than enthusiastic. When this happens, back off. There will be many more opportunities. There is no point in playing a game with a child if the game is not light-hearted, or if the child is not enjoying it. You may be disappointed if the child does not respond to your plans with the keenness you were hoping for, but don't let it show. There is always another time, another day. If you ever have to make a choice between your young child's happiness and the child's progress towards gaining another new skill, choose happiness. Do not let your own enthusiasm to make progress blunt your sensitivity to the child's state of mind. Whenever your child starts to feel anxious, pressured, conscious of displeasing you, or aware of failing to meet your expectations, learning stops being enjoyable. And when something ceases to be enjoyable the child will no longer be eager for more.

Compared with adults, young children are more easily distracted, more impatient, less good at attending and concentrating, and not so good at sitting still for long periods of time. They can quickly and suddenly get tired. Their moods may be quite unpredictable. And just when a parent thinks that a game is going marvellously, and the child is beginning to make exciting progress, the child may get tired of it, or decide that it would be more fun to run around and make a noise. At times like these it can be difficult for an enthusiastic parent to accept that the session is over: it may seem too much like 'giving in'. All the same, that is almost certainly the best thing to do. If in any doubt, stop. Knowing when to do so is important: otherwise the child's motivation to learn will almost certainly be damaged.

If possible, move on to another activity *before* the child gets tired with the first one. It is no tragedy if a game is left unfinished. Short sessions are sometimes more valuable than longer ones. There is no need to have a preconceived notion of how long a learning game or activity will last. Much can be learned from experiences that last no longer than thirty seconds, providing they are sufficiently frequent. It is important to avoid placing the child in a situation where he or she will be conscious of failing to do what is expected. It may take considerable time, and lots of practice, for a child to gain a new ability. Do not get impatient because progress is slower than you expected. Parents need to be sensitive about the kinds of feedback they provide, and sometimes it is better to let the child get on with an activity even if plenty of errors are being made, rather than constantly correcting. Do give lots of praise and plenty of encouragement. Let the child know that you are enjoying playing. If the child persists in making numerous errors, and you fear that these will impede learning, it is probably best to move to an easier task.

Some children have periods of being very negative, and at these times they may reject anything that the parents propose. On such occasions, when 'Shall I show you a new game?' or 'I know a good game: shall we play it?' yields a determined 'No', a less direct approach may be more effective. For instance, the parent might start playing the game alone, and the child might then become curious and start imitating. Or the materials might be left around for the child to discover.

## FURTHER READING

Baker, Carol. *Reading Through Play: The Easy Way to Teach Your Child*. London: Macdonald Educational, 1980.
Strongly recommended as an extremely down-to-earth and clear short guide.
Young, Peter, and Tyre, Colin. *Teach Your Child to Read*. London: Fontana, 1985.
Despite its title, this is not nearly as down-to-earth as Baker's book, but it gives an interesting and balanced account of various approaches to the teaching of reading.

These two books nicely complement each other: Baker's is more practical, but Young and Tyre's is informative and thought-provoking.

Chapter Seven

# The Origins of Exceptional Abilities

Some of the feats of outstanding individuals are quite dazzling. They are so remarkably superior to anything we can do ourselves that we simply cannot imagine how it is possible for any mortal person to achieve them. For instance, it is reliably reported that Mozart, after listening to two performances of Allegri's *Miserere*, was able to write out the complete score from memory. And as a child, Mozart was an astonishing prodigy. As well as being a singularly accomplished performer, he began composing music at the age of 5, wrote a symphony at 9, and his first opera at 13.

Why is it that a small number of people become extraordinarily able in one way or another? How do they get that way? The findings of research that was described in Chapter 2 provide strong evidence that when young children are given better-than-average opportunities to learn they make better-than-average progress. But how can we account for the achievements of those individuals whose abilities are the most impressive of all? These men and women have often enjoyed superior opportunities for early learning, but so have thousands of other people whose achievements are not at all remarkable.

When we read about the spellbinding feats of someone like Mozart, we feel almost compelled to believe that such a person must have been inherently different from ordinary individuals right from the day he was born. It seems hard to avoid concluding that Mozart, and other men and women whose achievements are similarly astounding, must have possessed innate aptitudes that the vast majority of people unhappily lack.

## EARLY BACKGROUNDS OF OUTSTANDING PERFORMERS

But some recent research findings suggest that such a conclusion might be mistaken. Lauren Sosniak, a psychologist, decided to investigate the early lives of twenty-four exceptionally able performing musicians (Sosniak, 1985, 1990). These were young American performers who had been stunningly successful, all having reached the finals of international piano competitions. Sosniak interviewed these outstanding pianists at some length, and also talked to their parents and to the teachers who had instructed them in early childhood.

The results of Sosniak's investigation contradict a number of widely accepted beliefs about exceptional musicians. For instance, whilst it is often assumed that those who are eventually outstanding display clear signs of being extraordinarily competent from a very early age, that was not true for most of the musicians whose early lives were investigated by Sosniak. The majority of them did not show unusual promise at the beginning of the long period of training and preparation that led, eventually, to their being so successful. For much of that time there were few indications that these individuals would go further than any of the thousands of other keen young musicians.

That is not to deny that these individuals were fairly impressive musical performers as children. They were, but in most cases they did not begin to be really exceptional until after they had become unusually committed to music and enthusiastic about it. By this time they were devoting unusual amounts of time to practising. So it appears that the eventual excellence of these pianists was at least as much an outcome as it was a cause of the intense interest and motivation that encouraged them to persevere at music.

So Sosniak's findings offer no support at all for the view that most of those performers who are eventually the most extraordinarily accomplished are individuals who have been exceptional right from the outset. In fact, she found that the identification of extraordinary skills occurred so slowly that the individuals were almost unaware of it happening. The period of training and preparation was very long: it took an average of seventeen years from the beginning of formal lessons for the pianists to gain their first international recognition. In some instances it was not until an individual had been working extremely hard for many years that people started to say that he or she was specially talented. For most of this time, in the majority of cases, it would have been quite impossible to predict that these particular individuals would eventually be anything like as successful as they actually became.

Sosniak's observations also fail to give support to another common belief, that outstanding musicians are usually people who have been born with 'perfect pitch' – a rare ability to discriminate between perceived auditory pitches. On close investigation this turns out not to be an innate ability after all, but a learned skill. It is most frequently acquired by children who begin their musical training when they are very young (Ericsson and Faivre, 1988), although with very careful training it has proved possible for an adult to acquire it (Brady, 1970).

As children, the individuals whom Sosniak studied were already outstanding, but their exceptionality lay less in their early achievements as such than in other qualities. They were most unusual in their degree of devotion to musical activities, exhibiting a remarkable willingness to persevere, year in, year out, at one highly specialized activity which made great demands on their time, their energy, and their concentration.

It is rare for a young person to possess the qualities it takes to persists so doggedly at an activity that is both demanding and narrowly channelled. What are these qualities? They seem to be ones that are only weakly governed by abilities as such. They appear to depend more on motivation, and on temperament and personality. Gaining an all-important sense of direction or purpose seems to involve the combination of particular abilities and these other attributes.

Where do these attributes come from? Why is it that a small number of young people are able to persist in their efforts at difficult specialized activities whilst most children seem to crave diversion and variety? That question is not at all easy to answer, but in the case of exceptional young musicians some clues are provided by Sosniak's insights into the family backgrounds of the individuals she studied. It is noteworthy, for instance, that in most cases even those parents who did not have strong musical interests themselves did all they could to ensure that their child was highly motivated to work at musical activities. The parents did not simply leave things to the piano teacher, but took on themselves the responsibility to make sure that the child practised regularly, by either sitting with or keeping an eye on the child during practice sessions. A third of the parents also sat in on most of the early lessons.

The piano teachers, too, were generally very effective at motivating the child musicians, particularly when they were very young. The first teachers were in some instances not at all technically impressive as musicians, but the majority of them were good at getting on with children and keeping them interested. Typically they were gentle, patient, and encouraging, and they obviously liked children. Often, they established warm, positive relationships with them.

A similar pattern of contributing factors has been observed in studies examining the causes of excellence in spheres of activity very different from music. That is to say, first, the levels of rewards and encouragement provided by parents and early teachers have been unusually high and, second, perhaps largely as a consequence, the children display a degree of willingness to persist at a particular demanding activity that is not at all characteristic of young people in general.

Both of these factors, unusual encouragement by parents and teachers and unusual persistence on the part of the young people, are highly typical of the circumstances in which a few young children who play tennis eventually become exceptionally able players who succeed at world championships. As in the case of the young musicians, it has been found that the tennis players had parents who were unusually willing to spend time with their child, giving help and encouragement in one form or another, or making a practice session into a game (Sloane, 1985). And the children were remarkably single-minded, even at periods of their early lives when their actual performance levels were not particularly remarkable.

## CAUSES OF GENIUS: INNATE TALENTS OR SPECIAL LIVES?

Findings broadly similar to Sosniak's observations emerge from each of a series of studies investigating the early lives of people who are outstanding at sports such as tennis (as we have seen) and swimming and diving, and at mathematics, the arts, and science (Sloane and Sosniak, 1985; Kalinowski, 1985; Monsaas, 1985; Gustin, 1985). More often than not, signs of remarkable promise right from the outset are conspicuously absent in those individuals who have eventually reached the peaks of success.

But what of a genius like Mozart? In the case of someone so totally exceptional as him, and especially in view of the fact that his abilities undoubtedly were remarkable at an early stage in his childhood, there seems to be no escaping the conclusion that he must have been born with some special gift or talent that other people lack. Is it not absurd to deny that he possessed some kind of natural aptitude that in some manner 'programmed' him for musical excellence? I am not so sure. Mozart was unarguably a composer of unique genius, but even with Mozart biographical information about his early life opens up the possibility that the exceptional opportunities he was given, and the exceptional childhood he led, go at least some way towards accounting for his exceptional achievements. He certainly was a capable performer at the piano from a very early age, and he did start composing when he was extremely young. But it is almost certainly wrong to believe that his achievements were quite so spontaneous or quite so effortless as popular accounts would have us think.

Our knowledge of Mozart's childhood is sketchy, but it is clear that his father, Leopold Mozart, an instrumentalist who was also an ambitious teacher of music, went to enormous lengths to ensure that the son became a successful musician. The single-minded Leopold, whose teaching of Mozart's older sister, Nannerl, had already been strikingly successful, 'dedicated much of his life to making his son into an important musician in the best way he knew' (Hildesheimer, 1983, p. 67). He strenuously promoted Wolfgang's career. The young Mozart had a very unusual childhood. There were few opportunities to play outdoors or to make friends with children of his own age. The chances are that, almost from the time he was born, a major part of the child's time was devoted to musical activities that were carefully directed by the father. Leopold was so ambitious for his son to succeed that when Wolfgang was no older than 6 the young prodigy and his sister were dragged around Europe on money-making tours. To advertise them Leopold designed posters which read like circus announcements. A clue to the degree of Leopold's determination to impress is provided by the fact that, to make the children's skills appear even more sensational than they really were, the poster announcements reduced their ages by one year.

Knowing how hard his father pushed him does nothing to alter the fact that the young Mozart was an exceptionally creative individual, but it does affect our efforts to explain how his genius might have been formed. We certainly cannot rule out the possibility that he was born with some kind of unique talent, but we are no longer compelled to accept this as the only conceivable explanation of his genius. There is no existing day-to-day record of the routine of Mozart's earliest days, and we have to guess at how his first years were actually filled. Yet we know enough to be certain that the experiences of a very unusual early childhood in which music was always present had a crucial influence.

But would that account for the remarkable memory feat I mentioned earlier, in which he speedily memorized (without even seeing it in musical notation) Allegri's score? Perhaps it would, if we bear in mind that the mature Mozart would have benefited from a musical education extending to at least twenty or thirty thousand hours. For him, the task would not have been anything like the feat it would represent for someone lacking an extensive musical education, namely that of being able to remember an exceedingly long series of separate notes or bars. For Mozart, what was being remembered would have been meaningful and significant in many different ways. He would not have had to recall individual notes separately because for him, as for other highly skilled musicians, considerably larger units would have been full of meaning. (For similar reasons, a church-goer who recalls the Lord's Prayer does not have to remember every individual letter.) It would have been quite unnecessary for him to memorize vast numbers of lower-level items (Sloboda, 1985).

As it happens, there exist a number of published reports showing that people who have spent a great deal of time studying particular kinds of information can often succeed at feats of memorizing that appear to be, and indeed are, quite impossible for a person who does not have that experience. For instance, chess masters are able to remember around fifty thousand separate chess positions (Chase and Simon, 1973).

To return to Mozart, even if his memory feats are not quite so totally inexplicable as they appear to be, and even if his exceptional childhood skills as a musical performer can be partly explained by the exceptional musical opportunities that his father arranged for him, how can we begin to explain the fact that he also *composed* – or so we are told – musical masterpieces when he was still a young child?

In this case the real facts are somewhat different from what has been widely reported. It is not actually true that Mozart composed great masterworks at the age of 5. As it happens, none of the compositions that are now regarded as being major works was actually written earlier than the twelfth year of his musical career (Hayes, 1981). That is to say, it was only after many years of rigorous training to be a composer that he began to produce his greatest music. Unique as Mozart was, like everyone else he needed a very long period of preparation in order to reach his highest levels of achievement. There were no short cuts, even for Mozart.

In an interesting investigation (Hayes, 1981), the same kind of analysis was done on the musical output of seventy-six other major composers. Hayes found that no more than three of the composers managed to produce major works before the tenth year of their composing career. (Incidentally, the three exceptions are Eric Satie, who produced *Trois Gymnopédies* in his eighth years as a composer, and Shostakovich and Paganini, who each composed a notable masterwork after nine preparatory years.)

The same applies to virtually all those individuals who create outstanding human achievements. Artists and writers, and scientists and mathematicians as well, reach the highest levels of competence only after many years of painstaking learning. The most striking feats depend on skills that demand thousands of hours of practice.

## THE IMPORTANCE OF PRACTICE

It is often remarked that 'mere practice' is not enough to enable exceptional skills to be acquired. That is true, up to a point, but many people underestimate its importance. They fail to recognize that, even if the amount of time which a person spends in enthusiastically practising a skill is not all-important, it is nevertheless an extremely powerful influence on a person's level of achievement.

Anders Ericsson and his colleagues (Ericsson *et al.*, 1990) have examined the role of practice as a determinant of the highest levels of achievement in three different areas of expertise: music, sports, and chess. In all three spheres these authors found that the amount of regular practice that a person does is an excellent predictor of the individual's level of success. The more the person practises, the better he or she performs. For instance, the achievements of young chess players are positively correlated with the amount of time they have devoted to the game. Similarly, sports players who regularly practice most and start training earliest outperform other players. In music, too, the most successful performers are those who practise most. Being an expert in any of these areas of ability demands extensive knowledge and high levels of skill, and the task of gaining these requires considerable time.

Of course, the fact that performance levels and time spent practising are correlated does not prove that more practice is straightforwardly the cause of better performance. It is possible that the correlations are partly due to the fact that the more successful performers simply enjoy lifestyles in which there are more opportunities for practising. However, the finding that practice and performance levels are correlated in a variety of different areas of skill, and at a number of different standards of expertise, makes it hard to avoid accepting the view that the amount of practice someone does is a crucial factor determining that person's level of achievement. But practice activities are not especially enjoyable. They demand effort and control and considerable repetition. Few young people want to spend lengthy periods of time, day after day, practising one particular skill. Most children would find that boring: they prefer variety and frequent changes of activity. A willingness to go on regularly practising for several hours every day is unusual, especially in children. So, although at first sight it would appear that what is most extraordinary about young people who are exceptionally skilled at playing the piano is their musical ability, on reflection what is more extraordinary is their willingness to dedicate so much time to arduous practice. The ability is certainly exceptional, but it is an end-product rather than a basic cause of a person's success. If we are interested in discovering what it is about an individual that makes it possible for them to *become* an exceptional musician, it might be sensible to investigate why people differ in the amount of time that they are willing and able to dedicate to the kinds of practice and preparation activities that are needed for reaching the highest levels of success in difficult areas of expertise.

The parents play a crucial role in helping a young person to gain the habit of regularly practising a time-consuming activity. Almost invariably, whenever a young person is seen displaying a high level of expertise at a difficult skill, we can be sure that parents or other adults will have done much to encourage the child and provide opportunities for training and practising. At the early stages, when the child is very young, the parents will typically have done their best to make the activity playful and enjoyable. They will have appreciated that young children do not find practising inherently motivating, and therefore cannot be expected to practise alone or without a great deal of support and encouragement. They will have praised the child's early efforts, and made sure that practising was rewarded. Later on, they will have helped to provide appropriate facilities for learning and practice, and will have helped to make sure that time for practising was made available within the child's daily routine. They will have encouraged the child to be aware of their own growing skills and to gain enjoyment and self-confidence from them, and perhaps a sense of identity as well, and to see themselves as someone with a special involvement in their field of expertise.

## EXCEPTIONAL INDIVIDUALS AND ORDINARY PEOPLE: ARE THEY TOTALLY DIFFERENT?

In this chapter I have suggested that when we are trying to discover how and why an exceptionally able individual has been capable of accomplishments that are greatly superior to those of other people, we should take care to avoid being too dazzled by the sheer excellence of their achievements. Otherwise it is easy to be led astray, and leap to the conclusion that, since the *feats* of a few remarkable people contrast so strongly with anything that ordinary people can do, the underlying causes are similarly distinct from the causes of ordinary people's abilities. Confronted by phenomena which seem inexplicable in any other way, we leap to the conclusion that certain exceptional people must have been born with special gifts or talents. Although there may be no positive evidence, we accept such a conclusion because there appears to be no alternative way of accounting for the most remarkable human achievements of all.

But, as our remarks about Mozart have demonstrated, such reasoning is flawed. In his case, closer examination of early circumstances suggested possible explanations for achievements which at first appeared to be quite inexplicable. There is no logical reason why the underlying causes of any human abilities, however stunning, need to be fundamentally dissimilar to the kinds of factor that would account for, say, my knowing more about literature than I know about mathematics, or for near-average Jill doing better at a geometry test than near-average Jack.

A simple illustration demonstrates how absurd it is to think that any human ability, however rare or exotic and however vastly it surpasses the capacities of other people, must depend on special innate talents or aptitudes.

In one investigation, some researchers encountered a young man who could remember lists of up to eighty random digits. After just one presentation of such a list he could recall it all, without any errors. As it happens, it is known that the maximum that most people can recall is around eight or nine items. It has also long been assumed that people's natural ability to retain items in memory is unchangeable. So there appears to be no way of avoiding the conclusion that this particular young man must have possessed a fundamentally exceptional capacity to remember. It is hard to think of any other reason for his ability to recall, as he could, ten times as much information as other people can.

But as it happens, we know that the person concerned was a quite ordinary student who was paid to participate in an experiment (Chase and Ericsson, 1981). He was required to practise recalling digit lists for an hour every day over a two-year period. When the experiment began, his performance was no better than average. His impressive achievement was the outcome of his being given exceptional opportunities to practise the skill.

It is unwise to assume that the causes of the stunning feats performed by 'exceptional' people must be fundamentally different from the causes of 'ordinary' people's abilities. The view that innate talents are necessary to account for exceptional skills – whether in music or sports, in science, mathematics, or the arts – is unjustified. This does not mean that we can entirely rule out the possibility that some exceptional people, such as Mozart, have been born with inherently special qualities or talents. But the research findings have established that such an explanation is not the only possible one. We can certainly question the assumption that it is essential to appeal to inherently special qualities whenever we seek an explanation of rare and remarkable human abilities.

In resisting the tendency to make such an appeal, the knowledge that feats which are rare in one culture are commonplace in another is especially valuable. In fact, certain accomplishments that are not at all uncommon in some cultures are virtually unknown in our own, and vice versa. So:

> the exceptionality of a performance lies in the eyes of the beholder. That is, we attribute to special gifts that which is rare and therefore seems beyond the reach of the average individual. The ability to interpret instantaneously very complex abstract symbols would seem to be an amazing accomplishment in a culture that had not developed written language. (Ericsson and Faivre, 1988, p. 452)

It would be wise to remember this statement when we read about the most exceptional feats of humankind. We are astonished by the amazing ability of aboriginal Australians to follow long, complicated routes over trackless and apparently featureless terrains (Lewis, 1976), or the marvellous capacity of Puluwat sailors to navigate miles of open water with no instruments. But while their everyday feats seem miraculous to us, some of our everyday activities would seem equally miraculous to them.

Chapter Eight

# *Child Prodigies*

The lives of child prodigies can tell us much about the underlying causes of exceptional abilities in young people, and about the consequences of a child's gaining skills and accomplishments that most people do not acquire until they are adults.

Child prodigies are adored by the media. It is hard to read a newspaper without confronting yet another story of some precocious child who has become a chess champion at a ridiculously early age, or gained a degree in mathematics, or won a tennis championship, or swum the English channel. A wave of publicity has greeted each of the achievements of Ruth Lawrence, who was first in the news in 1980, when she passed the British GCE O-level mathematics examination, and has since obtained degrees in mathematics (at 13) and physics. In 1986 another child, John Adams, passed the GCE A level Mathematics examination at the age of 9, an achievement that was matched in 1988 by Ganesh Sitampalam (Radford, 1990). In the spring of 1989 newspapers in Britain published numerous reports of three Hungarian sisters. The youngest, Judit Polgar, aged 12, was described as being the strongest ever chess player of her age, an achievement which is especially remarkable because it contradicts the notion, believed by many male chess players, that females are congenitally incapable of succeeding at the highest levels of the game.

For ordinary mortals like you and me, these accounts can make depressing reading. Beside them our own abilities and those of our children look puny. But what is the significance of being a prodigy in childhood? Why is it that a few children become prodigies? Do some of them arise 'out of the blue', with their families suddenly discovering that there is a prodigy in their midst? Or are child prodigies encountered only in the kinds of home in which the parents give their children a 'hothouse' early upbringing? For a person to become an outstandingly capable adult, is it necessary to have been a child prodigy? If not, is it helpful to have been one, or are child prodigies no more likely than ordinary children to become exceptional adults? Can being a child prodigy actually impede a person's chances of being a productive adult person, or make it hard for them to develop into a well-rounded and sociable individual? There do seem to be connections between being a child prodigy and being an exceptional adult. But for most people the actual form of the relationship between childhood precocity and mature achievement is not clear at all. And as we saw in the previous chapter, the most exceptional children do not always become the most exceptional adults. So finding out more about child prodigies – the lives they lead, and what happens to them when they get older – seems to be a promising way to add to our knowledge of the influences that contribute to outstanding abilities.

## FAMILY BACKGROUNDS

In this chapter I shall look at a few individuals who were prodigies as children. Their biographies provide some fascinating insights into the circumstances that lead to exceptional human accomplishments. These accounts can tell us about some of the ways in which a young person's early experiences affect the kind of adult person the individual eventually becomes.

The idea of a child genius suddenly appearing within a poorly educated family in which no one has made any special effort to stimulate the child's intellectual growth belongs more to fiction that to reality. I have examined some reports that seem to indicate that it can happen, but on close inspection the evidence they provide is never entirely convincing. In some cases it turns out that, despite superficial appearances, the child did receive a greater-than-average amount of encouragement, and did have unusual opportunities to learn. In other cases, especially ones in the fairly remote past, it is quickly apparent that there simply is not sufficient evidence to establish whether or not a childhood was actually as unstimulating and as barren of opportunities for learning as has been reported.

A complicating factor is the desire of certain eminent individuals to present their achievements as being largely self-made. Some autobiographical narratives exaggerate experiences of poverty or deprivation in childhood (Howe, 1982, 1990). For that reason, we should add a pinch of salt to Bernard Shaw's stories of rejection and neglect by an unloving mother. Or if we read H. G. Wells's fascinating autobiographical account of his early childhood, which harps on the squalor and poverty of those years, we should remember that his father was a voracious reader and something of a local celebrity, on account of his considerable success as a cricket player, and that his mother encouraged her child's early efforts to read by sticking on to objects in the house paper labels on which their names were written in large letters. That is hardly the act of a parent who was unconcerned – at least by nineteenth-century standards – about her child's early education.

It cannot be denied that the home environments of many child prodigies have been far from ideal. More than one future mathematician spent many hours working at the apparently unstimulating job of a shepherd. One of the great Victorian engineers, George Bidder, came from a family of penurious stonemasons. It was only as a result of his drawing attention to himself by performing remarkable childhood feats of mental arithmetic that he gained the sponsorship of wealthy individuals who were willing to finance the kind of education that made it possible for him to develop his abilities in directions that enabled him to become famous and successful.

Sadly, Bidder's example is all too rare. The kind of individual who comes from an impoverished and unlettered family background, but for whom doors are opened as a result of precocious accomplishments in childhood, is not at all typical of child prodigies. With the vast majority of prodigies the individual's exceptional abilities as a child were preceded by an unusual degree of willingness on the part of the parents to provide experiences and opportunities that encouraged early learning.

## JOHN STUART MILL

If there are 'typical' child prodigies, John Stuart Mill and Norbert Wiener would certainly qualify. Both were very exceptional children, and both subsequently became famous as a result of their intellectual achievements. Each wrote a detailed autobiographical account of his childhood years. And each of the two autobiographies clearly depicts both the advantages and the potential disadvantages of an intensive early education.

John Stuart Mill, born in 1806, was the son of James Mill, an enormously capable and energetic man who, despite having to provide for a wife and six children on a tiny income, took upon himself the immense labour of writing a lengthy (and highly esteemed) *History of India*. He also taught all his children. Being the eldest son, John Stuart's early education benefited from a considerably greater share of his father's attention than the other children received. Much of the responsibility for teaching the others was placed on John's shoulders, and it was a job he loathed.

James Mill taught his son at the same time as he was engaged on his own writing. The father and his children would sit together at a large table, and at intervals the father would look up from his labours in order to answer a question or correct his son's efforts, as the latter studied his lessons. John Stuart started Greek at the age of 3, learning from lists of Greek words and their English equivalents which his father had written on cards. Soon afterwards he worked on a Greek version of *Aesop's Fables*, and *The Anabasis*, but did not begin Latin until he was 7, by which time he had already mastered an impressive amount of literature in Greek, including 'the whole of Herodotus', works by Xenophon, Diogenes Laertius, Lucian, and Isocrates, and six of Plato's dialogues (the last of which 'I venture to think, would have been better omitted, as it was totally impossible I should understand it') (Mill, 1873, p. 5).

As a teacher, James Mill could be harsh, extremely demanding, sarcastic, and, as his son says, 'one of the most impatient of men'. Even so, James submitted to the constant interruptions of his own work that were made inevitable by the fact that the young John, often engaged beside him on his translation exercises to and from Greek, was unable to look up words for himself until he had started to master Latin, simply because lexicons for translating between Greek and English did not exist: the only Greek lexicons available at that time were Greek–Latin ones, and since the boy had no Latin he could use them only with his father's frequent assistance.

Every day, many of the young Mill's hours were devoted to lessons or reading (often from books borrowed from the library of his father's wealthier friend and mentor Jeremy Bentham). Arithmetic lessons – which the child strongly disliked – occupied the evenings. He knew hardly any boys of his own age, and never played games. He was allowed to amuse himself with true tales of adventures, and with books such as *Robinson Crusoe* and the *Arabian Nights*, but fairy stories were denied him, because James Mill disapproved of the morals they propounded.

It would not be totally wrong to say that John Stuart Mill had genius drummed into his head by the relentless efforts of his ambitious, never-resting father. Although John Stuart gained some remarkable abilities while he was still very young, James was convinced that his eldest son's mental powers were in no respect inherently unusual. He felt that the boy's ability to learn was no better than average. The son shared these views. In common with a number of exceptionally able individuals, including Albert Einstein and Charles Darwin, the younger Mill was convinced that he had no special intellectual gifts. Mill recorded in his *Autobiography*:

> From his [James Mill's] own intercourse with me I could derive none but a very humble opinion of myself . . . I was not at all aware that my attainments were anything unusual at my age . . . if I thought anything about myself, it was that I was rather backward in my studies, since I always found myself so, in comparison with what my father expected from me. (Mill, 1971, p. 33)

In contrast to the prevailing climate of opinion, which insisted that no one could possess mental abilities as exceptional as his unless they were born with innate advantages, Mill held to the view that extraordinary abilities result from extraordinary experiences and opportunities. He felt very strongly that the

> tendency to regard all the marked distinctions of human nature as innate, and in the main indelible . . . [in the face of 'irresistible proofs' to the contrary] is one of the chief hindrances to the rational treatment of great social questions, and one of the greatest stumbling blocks to human improvement. (Mill, 1971, p. 162)

Mill's *Autobiography* was published in 1873. Over a century later, the continuing malign influence of the beliefs that Mill had fought against prompted Stephen Gould to lament that 'few tragedies can be more extensive than the stunting of life, few injustices deeper than the denial of an opportunity to strive or even to hope, by a limit imposed from without, but falsely identified as lying within' (Gould, 1984, pp. 28–29).

## NORBERT WIENER

Norbert Wiener, born to Jewish parents in 1894, became one of the great mathematicians of the twentieth century. Intellectually, he was quite exceptionally precocious. When he was 11 he began an undergraduate course at Tufts College (now Tufts University) in Medford, Massachusetts. He graduated with a bachelor's degree at the age of 14. He was still 14 when he became a graduate student at Harvard, where he gained his doctorate at 18. After a period abroad, during which he worked with Bertrand Russell, he returned to the United States. In 1919 he was appointed to a post at the Massachusetts Institute of Technology. He stayed there for thirty-three years.

His father, like James Mill, was a scholar. Leo Wiener was an excellent philologist, and also had an extensive knowledge of mathematics and botany.

Leo Wiener had very definite ideas about the education of young children. He was very critical of the schools of the time: he was certain that the vast majority of children were capable of learning far more than schools normally teach. Also, like James Mill, he was sure that his own son possessed no special inherent gifts. The child was, Leo insisted, 'an essentially average boy who had the advantage of superlative training' (Wiener, 1953, p. 119).

From the start, Norbert's life was crammed with scholarly activities and intellectual stimulation. His father always shared his own intellectual interests with his family. The young Norbert had every encouragement to learn to read. His parents, who had many books in their house, encouraged their son to learn to read by himself when he was 3 years old. He soon became an avid reader, and devoured books on natural history, mathematics, and the physical sciences, as well as ones with more obvious appeal for a young child, such as *Treasure Island* and the *Arabian Nights*.

Leo Wiener was an extremely enthusiastic man who liked to talk about all of his many interests, but he was rather overbearing, too hot-headed and intense for most people's comfort, and, like James Mill, a hard taskmaster to his son. When Norbert was 7 his father decided to supervise his education throughout childhood, rather than leaving it to schools as most parents do. With the teaching of young Norbert in his father's hands, lessons could be just as tense and demanding as James Mill's had been. Wiener recalled:

> Every mistake had to be corrected as it was made. He would begin the discussion in an easy, conversational tone. This lasted exactly until I made the first mathematical mistake. Then the gentle and loving father was replaced by the avenger of the blood. The first warning he gave me of my unconscious delinquency was a very sharp and aspirated 'What!' and if I did not follow this by coming to heel at once, he would admonish me, 'Now do this again!' (Wiener, 1953, p. 67)

But although Leo Wiener was a domineering man and a demanding teacher, his son found much to admire in him. He taught Norbert botany and talked to him about farming, another of his many enthusiasms. Being a keen mycologist as well, he took his son on expeditions to collect fungi. And life in the Wiener household was intellectually stimulating in a number of other ways. A contributing influence was the fact that many of the family's friends and neighbours were scholars. Among his parents' friends were a number of leading intellectuals, including the physiologist Walter Cannon, who showed the child his newly developed X-ray machine and explained his work on the use of X-rays in the study of body tissues.

So, just as it is not altogether surprising that the highly concentrated programme of educational experiences that John Stuart Mill was obliged to submit to, day in and day out throughout his early years, produced a child who by mid-childhood was well ahead of his peers in those areas of knowledge and understanding that he had studied, it is equally unsurprising that the comparably intensive early education of Norbert Wiener made him unusually precocious in a variety of fields.

## THE SPECIFICITY OF HUMAN SKILLS

But in both Mill and Wiener precocious development was highly uneven, and restricted to certain particular realms of ability. In each case progress was accelerated only in those precise areas in which they had enriched opportunities to learn. Outside those areas of competence neither individual was at all superior. A similar developmental profile, with precocious abilities in certain restricted areas combined with progress that is not superior to the average at most other abilities, is typical in child prodigies. For instance, one study of 8-year-olds who were exceptionally advanced chess players found that they were perfectly normal in other spheres (Feldman, 1982). And the transcripts from the interview studies described in the previous chapter, in which exceptionally able young adults talked about their childhoods, are full of testimonies to the extreme ordinariness of those individuals, outside their particular areas of special talent (Bloom, 1985).

People often underestimate the degree to which results of learning are narrow and specific. From learning experiences we gain particular skills and particular items of knowledge. Generally, education does not teach us 'to think': it simply teaches us to think in particular ways about those topics on which we have received instruction. A failure to appreciate this has often resulted in unrealistic expectations, and in a consequent feeling of dismay when, say, a chess champion proves dim-witted in solving non-chess problems, or when a brilliant musician is discovered to be in no respect exceptional at dealing with non-musical aspects of life. It is even more shocking to discover that some high-ranking Nazi officials combined highly developed aesthetic sensibilities with the moral standards of barbarians.

We learn only what we learn, and child prodigies have sometimes become the objects of people's hostility when the false expectations of those who have failed to appreciate that fact have not been confirmed. A number of child prodigies have run into troubles caused by their failure to live up to the unrealistic expectation of teachers and other adults that their special abilities would be matched by comparable superiority in quite different areas of competence.

Norbert Wiener was strongly aware that even the most powerful thinkers can be glaringly ignorant outside their own areas of expertise. For all his precocious reading in the sciences, it was not until he was 7 that he discovered that Santa Claus does not exist. As he later reported,

at that time I was already reading books of more than slight difficulty, and it seemed to my parents that a child who was doing this should have no difficulty in discarding what to them was obviously a sentimental fiction. What they did not realize was the fragmentariness of the child's world. (Wiener, 1953, p. 81)

## THE PROBLEMS CHILD PRODIGIES CAN ENCOUNTER

So far as their sons' intellectual development was concerned, both James Mill and Leo Wiener were unquestionably successful. Both John Stuart Mill and Norbert Wiener were not only remarkably advanced in their intellectual development during childhood but also went on to become intellectual giants. Each has had a lasting influence on the field of scholarship with which he was associated.

But as I indicated in Chapter 3, as well as measuring the successes of a hothouse upbringing it is necessary to count the costs. For Mill and Wiener alike, the emotional costs of an unusual childhood appear to have been very considerable. They both experienced severe difficulties around the time that adulthood began. Although it is not possible to be absolutely certain of this, in all probability their troubles were directly caused, at least in part, by the exceptionally stressful circumstances of their early lives.

Mill fell into a severe depression at the age of 20. It lasted for about six months. Mill himself was quite sure that the cause of his depression lay in an education which sacrificed feelings and emotions to forms of thinking that were exclusively analytical. He began to appreciate that

the habit of analysis has a tendency to wear away the feelings: as indeed it has, when no other mental habit is cultivated, and the analysing spirit remains without its natural complements and correctives . . . to know that a feeling would make me happy if I had it, did not give me the feeling. My education, I thought, had failed to create these feelings in sufficient strength to resist the dissolving influence of analysis, while the whole course of my intellectual cultivation had made precocious and premature analysis the inveterate habit of my mind. I was thus, as I said to myself, left stranded at the commencement of my voyage, with a well equipped ship and a rudder, but no sail; without any real desire for the ends which I had been so carefully fitted out to work for. (Mill, 1971, pp. 137–139)

Mill's own explanation for his depression almost certainly places too much stress on the form and content of his education and too little on the influence of his domineering father. All the same, he was undoubtedly right to put his finger on the importance of a hothouse childhood in which exclusively intellectual qualities were forced at the expense of feelings.

Compared to Mill's, Wiener's difficulties were more drawn-out and diffuse. In his adolescence and early adulthood Wiener experienced troubles of many kinds, which left him frustrated, sometimes extremely depressed, and often in a mood of despair. There were elements of resentment, and a degree of self-pity. What he suffered from was less a crisis as such than a prolonged period of unhappiness, accompanied by a profound lack of self-esteem. It was in part a reaction to the contradictions and impossible demands of an intense, insecure, over-critical family, and partly the response of a young man who was painfully aware of his inadequacies and his lack of independence. As well as being clumsy and short-sighted, he found himself 'a confused, socially inept adolescent, who by any reasonable standard had been overworked for years and who needed every available moment to develop his social contacts and his social poise' (Wiener, 1953, p. 160).

It is rarely possible to be absolutely sure about causes and effects in the long-term course of people's lives, but it does seem extremely likely that important aspects of Wiener's life would have been easier for him had he not been so dependent on his parents or quite so aware of the demands of a father who expected a great deal from him. Extra difficulties were caused by the fact that the early development of his abilities was highly uneven. He was not at all socially assured. Mixing with his classmates at school and college, most of whom were several years older than him, was never easy for the young Wiener.

And it seems equally likely that, had James Mill been less harsh and joyless, or a less grimly demanding father, his brilliant son would have been a warmer, more engaging, and perhaps happier adult. He might not have experienced the deep depression that almost drove him to suicide at the age of 20.

Yet it is worth emphasizing again that we cannot be at all certain that the emotional difficulties and other problems of adjustment that both Mill and Wiener experienced as young adults were caused by the circumstances of their early lives, unusual (and somewhat harsh, in Mill's case) as these were. Unhappiness and neuroticism are certainly not unknown in individuals who have not received any kind of hothouse education in early life. Even if we accept that part of the blame must lie with the over-demanding fathers, it is still not possible to be sure that the intense early educational experiences as such were a major cause of subsequent difficulties. In both families there were a number of different factors that might have contributed to making the transition to adulthood especially traumatic. For example, Mill was keenly aware that his mother gave him only limited love and support. And in Wiener's family there were various stresses and strains in addition to the ones that directly attended the unusual early education he experienced.

Within the family Wiener was for some years in the position of being intellectually mature but treated like a child. He was dependent on his parents, with no independent means of his own, and was given plenty of responsibilities but little authority. Throughout his life he remained bitter about having been saddled with the job of teaching his younger brother. Actually, as he must have realized when he came to read Mill's *Autobiography*, compared with Mill, who had to teach several of his siblings, Wiener escaped very lightly in this respect. But it was the kind of situation in which it is easy to understand the 16-year-old Norbert longing 'for the beginning of term to relieve me from the boredom which came from a family living too close together and driven in upon itself' (Wiener, 1953, p. 157).

Broadly speaking, however, it seems fair to conclude that the kinds of family in which parents not only place enormous emphasis on early education but also make it clear that they expect much from their children are often families in which it is unusually difficult for a young person to make the kinds of transition that are necessary in order to grow up and become a fully independent adult. Mill and Wiener apart, it is not difficult to find instances of emotional stress that appear to have originated in the intense family atmospheres that are prone to be created by parents who place great store on their children's success. Another well-known individual whose remarkable abilities first emerged when he was very young was John Ruskin. The atmosphere of his home appears to have been as demanding as Mill's and as claustrophobic as Wiener's; he also experienced a severe crisis at the beginning of adult life, and recurring breakdowns in later years.

## SOME ANSWERS AND CONCLUSIONS

At the beginning of the chapter I raised a number of questions about child prodigies, some of which can now be answered. Hothouse early educations do, at least in some instances, lead to remarkable intellectual precocity. Some child prodigies undoubtedly do become outstanding adults. But in some cases at least, early hothousing, or certain aspects of the family backgrounds that often accompany it, can appear to be a source of stress that leads to unhappiness and depression. These problems may be severe enough to prevent individuals from making productive use of their abilities.

Mill and Wiener both survived their crises, though the scars of their difficult childhoods remained with them. But other hothoused prodigies, such as William Sidis, a friend and contemporary of Wiener, were less fortunate. Sidis, the brilliant child of a father who was no less committed to giving his son a hothouse education than Leo Wiener was, became just as exceptional a child as Wiener (Wallace, 1986). But his social limitations were even more marked than Wiener's, and an account of his home life reads like a caricature of the other's. Sidis's father seems to have been even more demanding than Leo Wiener. The adult life of William Sidis was rather a sad one. He never made effective use of his remarkable intellectual skills. He earned a meagre living from jobs that involved limited responsibility.

Can a person become an exceptionally able adult without having been a child prodigy? The answer is definitely positive, though the proportion of intellectually outstanding adults who have not been somewhat precocious in childhood is surprisingly small. Charles

Darwin was one great scientist who, as a boy, was not thought to have been at all remarkable. Although he was bright, and throughout his childhood very interested in biological pursuits, it was not until he was around twenty that people started to look on him as an especially capable individual.

But the majority of individuals who have achieved eminence in later life as a result of their intellectual achievements were certainly advanced for their age when they were children. We should not make the mistake of assuming that unless a person was described at the time as a child prodigy, it would be safe to infer that the individual's abilities were not above average. The chances are that among the many great scientists, scholars, artists, poets, dramatists, and novelists whose parents and teachers did *not* see in them any special qualities, many did nevertheless possess exceptional abilities in childhood.

Take the case of Albert Einstein. No one called him a prodigy when he was young; and because he did not shine at school, and failed to pass an important examination, it has been suggested that he was a child of less-than-average ability. But in fact, by the age of 12 he was reading serious books on the physical sciences and was also an enthusiastic and extremely precocious mathematician. At 16 he wrote a brilliant paper on electromagnetic phenomena, 'Concerning the Investigation State of Aether in Magnetic Fields'. In this work it is possible to see the beginnings of interests that eventually led to monumental achievements.

If it is not essential to have been a child prodigy to achieve eminence later in life, does it help? In most instances it definitely does. It is unusual nowadays to encounter the state of affairs in which a child from a poor background has precocious skills which bring the individual to the attention of those who can provide educational opportunities that would not otherwise be available. But there are still a number of fields in which scarce or expensive resources are likely to be made available only to an individual who has made extraordinary progress by an early age. Financial restrictions still prevent many young people – even the quite brilliant – from having access to advanced education, especially in the Third World. For example, the remarkable Indian mathematician Srinivasa Ramanujan was acknowledged to be a child prodigy of immense ability but was nevertheless denied the support necessary for him to have received higher education.

To become a top-ranking concert pianist the young performer needs to have tuition from one of a very small number of distinguished master teachers. But these individuals are prepared to offer their services only to pupils whom they consider to be unusually promising. So finding such a teacher is a hurdle that can be surmounted only by a young person who is already extremely accomplished. Similarly, to become a world-class tennis player it is necessary to practise all year, and a young player can expect to meet fierce competition for the funds that exist to help make this possible.

On the whole, the richer one is, the less essential it is to be a prodigy at the beginning of one's life. Wealthy individuals have always been to some extent immune from the necessity to make career choices while they are still very young. For instance, Leo Tolstoy, a rich man who could always afford to pay his gambling debts, could sample a variety of occupations before settling down in his forties to write novels. William James depended on his father's wealth while he vacillated for several years before deciding to spend the rest of his life studying philosophy and psychology. Charles Darwin was doubly fortunate: not only was his father wealthy, but the strong continuities between his childhood interests and his adult fields of study compensated for the lack of strikingly precocious early skills.

Finally, being unusually precocious can increase the chances of eventual success in a quite different way. There are some fields of scholarship in which each of the following two conditions exist. First, it is vital to maintain a single-minded commitment over a period of many years in order to reach the highest levels of excellence. Second, it is unlikely that such a commitment will endure into the middle years of life, largely because even the most wholeheartedly dedicated of individuals will eventually begin to look outside a particular narrow pursuit, and to take more interest in other concerns, such as family matters. In these circumstances, major achievements are most likely to be made fairly early in life. Mathematicians, for example, tend to produce their best and most important work in their twenties and thirties. For it to be possible to reach one's peak by this time it is vital to have already gained a high level of expertise by around the late teens. For this reason, an early start is virtually essential.

# Chapter Nine

# The Nature of Human Abilities

Although children's abilities have been a central concern in each of the chapters of this book, almost nothing has been said about the actual nature of human abilities. Knowing something about the forms that abilities take can be helpful when it is necessary to make practical decisions about how best to help young people to extend their spheres of expertise and competence.

'Ability' is a common word. It is very widely used. If someone can run a mile in less than five minutes, we describe that person as having exceptional athletic ability. If a child does not read as well as most children, we say that he or she lacks reading ability. A child prodigy who can solve complex problems in mathematics is said to have exceptional mathematical ability.

But what exactly *is* an ability? It is possible to answer the question by saying that an ability is a potential to do something, or a capacity, but all that does is to exchange one word for another. It is just as hard to specify exactly what we mean by a potential or a capacity. Most attempts to define abilities involve circular thinking. This is apparent when we ask how one knows that someone has an ability. The usual answer to that question is that the person can do something. So all that is really being said by the statement that a person has ability is that the person has whatever it takes to do some specified task. A similar circularity of thought is evident whenever the concept of ability is introduced to explain people's actions. If I say, for example, 'she reads well because she has high reading ability', all that is actually being stated is that she reads well because she possesses the attribute of being able to read well.

Words that are familiar and widely used are often assumed to mean something more precise than they actually do. 'Ability' is one such word. It is worth repeating that, in saying that an ability exists, all that is being done is to draw attention to a state of being able to do something. The statement does not explain why or how it is done. What governs a person's abilities? How are the different abilities interrelated, organized, and controlled? These are practical questions that we need to be concerned about if we are seriously interested in extending and improving people's abilities, especially those of young children. Our decisions about making practical interventions aimed at adding to young people's accomplishments are largely governed by the ways in which we think about abilities. If our thinking is faulty, it is more than likely that our practical efforts will be misdirected, and consequently ineffective.

## ARE ABILITIES AUTONOMOUS?

It is well known that people who are good at some skills tend also to be good at other skills that are similar. So, for instance, if young children in a school classroom are ranked for their performance at an arithmetic test and also ranked for their scores on a test of reading, the ranked scores will be positively correlated. That is, there will be a tendency for those children who do best at the reading test to do well also at the arithmetic test. There will be a similar tendency for those who do badly at one test to perform poorly at the other.

Findings of this kind have encouraged the widespread assumption that a person's different intellectual abilities are to some extent centrally controlled. It is often believed, for instance, that everyone possesses a certain amount of intelligence, and that a person's intelligence level constrains that individual's various abilities. If that were true, it would follow that someone who lacked sufficient general intelligence would be unable to master a course in, say, advanced mathematics.

This view of abilities seems plausible enough. It is widely accepted by psychologists and teachers. However, there are strong grounds for arguing that it is totally wrong and that particular abilities are considerably more independent than that view implies.

There are at least two kinds of possible constraint on the extent to which a particular ability may be independent or autonomous. First, the likelihood of someone being able to acquire one ability may depend on whether or not they possess certain other abilities. Second, this likelihood may depend on the extent to which they possess some essential central capacity, or 'intelligence'.

There are practical reasons for wanting to know to what extent a person's abilities are constrained by these factors. The degree to which they are will largely determine the answers to practical questions concerning whether or not all individuals are capable of acquiring any particular learned ability. Conceivably, certain abilities can be acquired only if the individual already possesses attributes or qualities that are totally outside the teacher's control. For instance, it might be quite impossible for Jack to be taught to read because he is not sufficiently intelligent. In that case, it would be not only pointless but also cruel to put Jack through a lengthy series of experiences designed to teach him reading. Similarly, if the accelerated progress and other benefits that are said to result from hothousing are in fact only available to those children who happen to possess certain inborn attributes, it would be futile and unkind to submit other children to special early learning experiences. So we need to know to what degree it is possible for *any* child to acquire exceptional capabilities, irrespective of any inherent attributes that the child happens to possess. The findings of research described in Chapter 2 went some way towards establishing that the vast majority of children are in fact capable of profiting immensely from having enriched opportunities to learn. But to be sure about this we also need to have information concerning the extent to which various abilities are autonomous.

## EVIDENCE OF AUTONOMOUS SKILLS

To what extent, then, are human abilities independent, separate, and autonomous? There is a substantial amount of factual evidence on this matter. It points to the conclusion that different abilities are independent to a much higher degree than is normally believed.

In Chapter 8 I mentioned some anecdotal evidence indicating that skills of prodigies can be surprisingly fragmentary. Apparently, it is possible for people to be remarkably accomplished at one particular skill and at the same time totally incompetent at others, even ones that would appear to involve similar or related fields of expertise. There are numerous anecdotes about dim-witted chess masters and famous scientists who find it difficult to cope with everyday tasks such as dressing themselves, but they hardly amount to hard scientific evidence. However, there are plenty of more solidly-based findings which demonstrate that particular areas of ability are indeed largely autonomous, in some people at least.

In the first place, there is a large body of evidence demonstrating that in certain mentally handicapped people (usually known as 'idiots savants') extraordinarily high levels of ability in certain restricted areas of competence can coexist with profound mental retardation (Howe, 1989). For instance, there are case histories of individuals who are outstanding musicians and yet totally incapable of looking after themselves or conducting even a minimally coherent conversation. There are people who can perform breathtaking feats of mental arithmetic, or calculations that make it possible to specify the day of the week for a calendar date in the remote future, but cannot understand the meaning of simple sentences. Some individuals can remember the details of every news bulletin for years but cannot read or write. And there are children who have an unparalleled ability to draw accurate and realistic pictures of the visual world but are unable to use language and communicate with other people.

Of course, these individuals are rare. Because they are, it is tempting to dismiss them as anomalies. We can try to persuade ourselves that their extreme patterns of contrasting abilities and disabilities are irrelevant to an understanding of ordinary people. But I don't think that such feats can be so easily ignored. The observation that there are some people in whom superior and inferior abilities clearly do coexist tells us that it definitely is possible for various kinds of ability to exist in relative isolation. In people of average intelligence we do not usually encounter the same sharp contrasts between levels of competence at different spheres of activity, but this does not mean that they *cannot* occur.

There are additional kinds of evidence indicating that different abilities are separate, and independent of one another, to a greater extent than is normally believed. Research into the effects of brain damage is one source of such evidence. If two different skills that a person happens to possess are interdependent, we would expect to find that brain damage that eradicates one of these skills will also affect the other skill. But if the skills are autonomous, we should find that it is possible for brain damage to destroy one skill while leaving the other intact. Knowing the extent to which it is possible for a particular ability to remain intact while other abilities (similar ones in particular) are destroyed provides useful information concerning the degree of autonomy in human abilities.

The research findings are extremely interesting. They show that it is indeed quite possible for certain abilities to be completely destroyed as a result of brain damage, while other abilities, even highly similar ones, remain entirely intact. For example, damage in the part of the left hemisphere known as Broca's area can lead to a person's speech being reduced to the utterance of very short and simple phrases, while that person is still reasonably successful at understanding language. People who have suffered damage to a different part of the left hemisphere, Wernicke's area, retain the ability to speak fluently and in complex grammatical sentences, but the content and meaning is liable to be unclear. Lesions in a third part of the brain, the angular gyrus, lead to a specific inability to locate particular words and names, so that speech is filled with terms like 'kind of', 'things', and 'stuff'.

After brain damage, someone may be able to understand a request to do certain actions, and also physically capable of doing so, but unable to carry out those actions in the correct sequence. Drawing, calculating, and certain finger skills may be lost while other intellectual abilities stay undamaged. A brain-injured person may suffer total loss of memory for language and verbal materials and yet retain the capacity to remember large amounts of complex information in the form of physical behaviours. As a result, a person may be able to carry out a sequence of complicated activities that must have been remembered from previous occasions, but at the same time deny that the activities have ever occurred before. Some people lose the ability to use language but can do calculations and simple arithmetic; others retain language but lose calculating skills. Sometimes, people who have suffered brain damage retain the ability to identify numbers and do arithmetic but cannot read verbal items that surround the numbers. One individual could identify DIX as the roman number for 509, but could not read the same letter sequence as a language syllable (Gardner, 1984).

## EFFECTS OF TRAINING: GENERAL OR SPECIFIC?

These and other effects of brain damage show that different abilities can be remarkably specific. Further evidence about the separateness and autonomy of particular skills comes from studies in which someone has been trained to master a particular skill. To what extent does the outcome of such training transfer or generalize, so that the individual is then able to succeed at tasks other than the ones specifically trained? Research findings indicate that the effects of training may be considerably more specific than is generally realized.

For instance, you may recall the individual, described in Chapter 7, who was trained over a two-year period to retain lengthy sequences of digits. Eventually, the level of his performance at this particular task was extremely impressive: he could correctly recall lists of digits that were many times as long as the lengthiest lists other people can remember. But, after all the training he received, how well could he recall other kinds of material? What was he like at remembering, for instance, lists of words, or narratives in prose or verse? In other words, to what extent had his training resulted in a general improvement in ability to remember? The answer to that question is very clear. Not in the slightest! At the end of his training, despite his phenomenal ability at the task he had practised, he was no better than the rest of us at other memory tasks. For all the training he had received, he did not gain 'a good memory'. He simply had impressive ability to perform a particular memory feat.

## IS GOOD MEMORY AN ILLUSION?

This raises the question of how a good memory is acquired. If all the training the young man received over a two-year period did not succeed in giving him a good memory, what would? Or is a good memory something that you happen to be born with (or without)?

The fact of the matter is that the question is based on an illusion. There is no such thing as a good or a bad memory. All that we possess are specific memory skills. Almost everyone is good at remembering certain things, and not so good at remembering others. Broadly speaking, we are good at remembering those events and items about which we are highly knowledgeable and which we regard as being important to us, those things in which we are interested and in which we have had a fair amount of practice at learning and remembering. We are not good at remembering those things about which we know little or in which we have little interest or experience, or which we find hard to understand.

It may seem rather outrageous for me to insist that there is no such thing as a 'good memory'. After all, most people share this way of thinking about the cause of success or failure at remembering. How can it possibly be illusory? There is no denying the fact that some people remember things more accurately than others, so what is wrong with describing someone who remember things well as someone who has a good memory?

What is wrong with that description quickly becomes clear if we ask each of a number of people to attempt a substantial number of different memory tasks. We would expect to find – if we believe that the concept of a good memory is valid – that there are some people who perform well at most or all the tasks, and some people who do badly at most or all of them. The former individuals could then be described as having good memories, and the latter as having bad memories. In fact, however, it turns out that we do not find any people who fit either of these patterns. That is to say, there are no people who perform uniformly well or uniformly poorly at a variety of different memory tasks. Knowing how well someone has performed at any one memory task tells us nothing about how that individual will do at a different task.

The same applies to learning. Just as it is wrong to imagine that people can be classified as having good or bad memories, it is equally erroneous to think that people are good or bad at learning in general. Generally speaking, someone who already knows a lot and has acquired a substantial number of cognitive skills will have more success at learning tasks than a person who lacks those qualities. But that is not because the first individual is better equipped with some kind of general learning ability: the difference lies in specific kinds of mental skill and knowledge that the first person possesses. If that person is faced with a new learning task for which he or she is not already equipped with appropriate knowledge or mental skills, performance will be no better than average. That fact of life has surprised many a bright student who wished to learn to drive a car.

## WHY SKILLS ARE CORRELATED

Together, the different kinds of evidence convincingly show that abilities are largely independent and autonomous. But if abilities are independent, why is there any tendency at all for a person's levels of performance at different skills to be correlated? Why is it that those children who are good at reading tend to be better than average at arithmetic? Is there not a paradox here? How can abilities be both independent and correlated?

An answer is that a person's level of performance in different areas of ability will be correlated when, but only when, either or both of two conditions exist. The first is that the two abilities draw upon the same knowledge or skills. For instance, if children are given a series of addition tasks and a series of multiplication tasks, the chances are that those children who do well at the additions will also do well at multiplying, simply because the two kinds of task share common elements. As a result, performance at the two kinds of task will tend to be correlated.

The second condition is that the acquisition of the two abilities draws on particular personal attributes that will affect an individual's degree of success at both of them. What are these attributes? They are numerous, and include qualities more closely related to personality, temperament, motivation, and personal style than they are to abilities as such. For example, the degree to which a person will succeed at each of a range of different abilities may depend to some extent on how competitive the individual is, and how self-confident, how attentive, reflective, dogged and persevering, resistant to distractions, and patient.

## THE AUTONOMY OF ABILITIES: SOME IMPLICATIONS

The adequacy of our ideas about the nature of abilities is crucially important when we need to know how best to respond to practical challenges. Let's assume that Johnny is having trouble learning to read. Essentially there are two ways of confronting this problem.

If we believed that particular abilities are not at all independent, and that what people achieve largely depends on factors such as 'general ability', good memory, or intelligence level, we would be inclined to respond in the following way. We might say that Johnny is not clever enough, or insufficiently smart, or lacking in intelligence, that he 'lacks ability', or suffers from 'learning disability' or 'dyslexia'.

In practice, introducing these labels achieves very little: for all down-to-earth purposes we might as well just shrug our shoulders and say that Johnny is the kind of child who has trouble learning to read. Such a fatalistic attitude is far too common. Many people, including some teachers, use language of this kind when confronted by a child's failure to learn. And if the facts and the logic justified this kind of response there would be no alternative to a somewhat fatalistic acceptance of the situation.

But, as I have shown, neither the facts nor the logic justify that kind of response. The evidence that demonstrates the autonomy of human abilities indicates that we should take a very different attitude to failure, and a much more active one.

The alternative response is necessary because it achieves what the above reaction clearly fails to do. First, it directs our attention to the actual causes of difficulty. Second, it points towards real solutions, in the form of practical steps that can be taken for overcoming difficulties. We might start by bearing in mind that there must be specific reasons for Johnny's failure. (Statements like 'lack of learning ability' or 'poor memory' are not reasons at all: they are labels masquerading as reasons.) Next, we might proceed to consider what might be lacking. What is preventing Johnny from reading? What possible obstacles could be getting between him and the goal of learning to read fluently? Perhaps he lacks certain skills that reading depends on. As we saw in Chapters 2 and 6, such an explanation is essentially correct in many instances of failure to read. Perhaps he lacks particular elements of knowledge, such as knowledge of letter–sound correspondences.

Perhaps Johnny is not very interested in learning to read. If he never sees anyone in his family reading, he may never have learned to think of reading as a useful or desirable skill to have. Perhaps he has never learned to concentrate or reflect in the ways that are necessary for coping with a task such as reading. He might be bright and quick in his reactions. These are qualities that are often valuable in life, but which, in order for someone to succeed at school, need to be supplemented by the capacity to concentrate attention and reflect on things. Children from relatively bookish homes will have experienced many opportunities for cultivating these qualities long before the beginning of schooldays, but Johnny may have missed out.

Perhaps Johnny has emotional problems. Possibly he has anxieties which prevent him concentrating effectively on school tasks, and these anxieties may have been strengthened by his own school failures.

The possibilities are almost endless. The important point is this: so long as one sees learning successes and failures as reflections of generalized, centrally controlled qualities that underlie all human abilities, one is forced to conclude that very little can be done to increase or accelerate learning in most young children. As soon as we discard that viewpoint, we escape the fatalistic conclusions that it leads to. We can then take the far more effective down-to-earth approach of looking for the particular reasons for a person's success or failure at acquiring a particular ability. Following up the implications of this approach will not always be easy, of course. But as soon as we begin to acknowledge that different abilities are largely autonomous, and are acquired only in certain specific circumstances, we can start to bring about the conditions in which an individual will be able to gain a desired capability.

## INTELLIGENCE AND HUMAN ABILITIES

Up to now I have said little about the concept of intelligence. This may seem surprising, in view of the ubiquity of the term. It is virtually certain to be introduced in a discussion of those abilities that are in any respect intellectual in form. You cannot, apparently, be good at mathematics, or science, or literature, without being intelligent. In that case, is it not true to say that intelligence is fundamental to abilities? And is it not also true that the concept of intelligence is central to our understanding of human abilities?

Up to a point. But both assertions partly rest on misconceptions about the actual nature of human abilities. Consider first what we mean by 'intelligence'. Imagine we are comparing two men. One of them is noticeably better than the other at coping with a variety of situations that involve cognitive capabilities such as thinking, reflecting, solving problems, answering general knowledge questions, learning, mental arithmetic, and so on. Generally speaking, he is more effective at mental tasks of various kinds.

Our language has a number of terms for describing this superiority. We might say that the first individual is brighter, smarter, quicker, wiser, sharper, more astute, cleverer, or more intelligent. In everyday life these terms – which are to some extent interchangeable – are all useful. Everyone knows what we mean by them. They *describe* what people are like, so far as their mental abilities are concerned. On the basis of these descriptions we can make helpful predictions about what individuals are likely to be able to do.

Furthermore, it is possible to construct tests which can give us an indication of how bright or smart or intelligent an individual is. Such tests can be very useful. For example, if someone without formal qualifications applies for a job that demands an ability to do mental calculations, or applies to take a course of instruction leading to an academic qualification, it might be helpful to have an indication of how well the individual is likely to cope with various intellectual challenges. Not surprisingly, a large number of such tests have been devised, and they are regularly used for a variety of purposes. They could have been called smartness tests, or cleverness tests, or brightness tests. As it happens, they are usually referred to as intelligence tests. Although they have aroused a variety of controversies, few would deny that such tests have their uses.

## A PURELY DESCRIPTIVE CONCEPT?

As an everyday concept to describe people who are generally good at intellectual tasks and problems, and as a term to describe practical tests, there are few grounds for objecting to the use of the word 'intelligence'. But its use does become exceptionable when, instead of introducing it solely to help *describe* individuals' capacities, people start to make use the concept in ways that are intended to provide scientific *explanations* of what an individual can achieve. For instance, a person might be said to be good at mathematics 'because she is intelligent', or it might be said that high abilities 'originate in intelligence' or that intelligence is 'fundamental' to certain intellectual abilities. When the terms are used in these ways, there is an assumption that intelligence is not simply a descriptive term, but also some kind of quality, essence, entity, or 'thing', which underlies, and is therefore fundamental to, different abilities.

These uses of 'intelligence' are invalid and misleading. They are examples of the kind of crooked thinking that is known as 'reification'. To reify a concept is to take an adjective that has a descriptive function, turn it into a noun, and then assume that the noun must refer to some concrete thing. For example, think of the word 'productive'. It is a useful adjective, and if we want a way to compare two factories it may be helpful to be able to say that one factory is more productive than another. There is nothing to object to here. And if we wish, we can also speak of the 'productivity' of a factory. Again, this is unobjectionable. But it would be totally illegitimate to use the word 'productive' as an explanatory rather than a descriptive term. For instance, if I were to say that one factory produces more goods than another 'because it is more productive', I would be talking nonsense. All I would be saying, in effect, is that the first factory produces more goods because it is the kind of factory that produces more goods.

Roughly the same situation exists when 'intelligence' is used in ways that purport to describe abilities, as when it is said that high intelligence causes, explains, or is fundamental to abilities, or that abilities originate or have their roots in high intelligence.

Some of these difficulties might be avoided if it were possible to *define* intelligence unambiguously and construct tests based on that definition. But this has never been done. Many people have provided their own definitions of intelligence, but every definition is different, and all of them are much too vague to form the basis for constructing test items. Largely for this reason, people devising intelligence tests have taken little notice of definitions and have tended to choose items on a purely practical basis. If a test item is effective for predicting someone's performance, it is likely to be chosen. There is nothing fundamentally wrong with this procedure, providing that the test is intended for purely practical purposes. But if you try to answer the question 'What is an intelligence test actually measuring?', you will fail. There is no specific definition of intelligence to which the test items correspond. So all that can be said is that the test measures how people perform the tasks that are set in the test.

It is sometimes said that 'intelligence is what intelligence tests measure'. This is a fair statement, but, since different intelligence tests measure different things, it is also a meaninglessly vague statement. A concept that cannot be clearly defined can play only a limited role in scientific explanation. So when we say that intelligence is fundamental to abilities, or that abilities are rooted in or originate in intelligence, or are being controlled or constrained by it, the meaning is not at all precise. All we can really mean is that 'something that we cannot precisely define or specify' is fundamental to abilities, or provides their origins or roots. It is only too clear that nothing at all is being explained.

Because intelligence is not the objectively defined explanatory concept it is often assumed to be, it is more an obstacle than an aid to understanding abilities. There is no harm in simply *describing* a person as intelligent (or smart, or clever, or bright, for that matter). But the widespread belief that everyone possesses some mysterious quality of intelligence to a greater or lesser degree, and that the extent to which an individual has that quality determines how well or how poorly they will perform, is totally wrong and highly misleading. If we wish to help young people extend their abilities, rather than using the concept of intelligence in this way we might be wiser to abandon it altogether.

Chapter Ten

# Genes, Natural Gifts, Innate Talents: Fact and Fiction

Why aren't humans identical clones of one another, like Coca-Cola bottles? Everybody knows that there are two main causes of variability between individuals. First, people are not genetically identical. Second, they do not grow up in identical environments. Many efforts have been made to disentangle the effects of these two kinds of influence and to decide on the relative importance of each. Despite many misunderstandings and confusions, much progress has been made.

Controversies about the effects of inherited and environmental influences have generated a great deal of heat. For well over a century there have been scientists firmly committed to the view that people's abilities are largely determined by hereditary factors, and others equally strongly committed to the belief that people's differing environments are a more important cause of variations in ability. It has often seemed to outsiders that the battle has been fought along lines that are as much political as scientific, with broadly conservative writers identifying with the hereditarian cause, and socially progressive individuals embracing the environmental one.

## MISUNDERSTANDINGS ABOUT GENETIC CAUSATION

As it happens, there is abundant evidence that inherited characteristics do affect human abilities, but the implications of this are by no means as gloomy as anti-determinists have sometimes thought them to be. Contrary to what both supporters and opponents of the hereditarian view have believed, the fact that a trait is partly inherited does not usually rule out the possibility of it being radically modified by environmental influences. The common view that genes provide firm blueprints that directly and immutably determine abilities is totally false. There is nothing at all inevitable about the effects of hereditary influences on psychological characteristics. Our fortunes are not set out in advance by our genetic make-up. A simple example serves to illustrate this crucial point. It shows that, paradoxical as it may seem, appropriate changes in the environment can have enormous effects on abilities that are determined by genetic factors.

Let us imagine that it has just been discovered that a genetic cause underlies differences between children in the ease with which they can learn to read. But no one yet understands the nature of the genetic mechanism involved, and we do not know how its effect is exerted. So it is widely assumed that there is no way of helping the poor readers. Because the cause is known to be genetic, it appears that their fate is sealed, and nothing can be done about the matter: it seems, at first, that these children are born to be illiterate. But a few years later scientists discover that the genetic influence is exerted via the visual processes. Quite simply, some children find it easier than others to identify letters of the alphabet. This source of variability leads, in turn, to differences in children's rate of success at learning to read. Once this further discovery has been made, it is immediately clear that these differences, despite their genetic origins, can easily be eliminated by an appropriate environmental modification. All that needs to be done is to provide spectacles for those children who cannot see so well. Once that is done, the differences disappear. In other words, the effect of an environmental modification (providing the children with spectacles) is to eliminate the (genetically caused) difference between the groups in ability to read.

Usually, the ways in which genetic causes affect human abilities are not quite so straightforward as in this example. All the same, it is likely that in the majority of instances there is an equivalent degree of openness to environmental modification. The outcomes of genetic differences between people are not immutable. One reason is that the effects of genes on abilities are normally indirect rather than direct. Typically, genetic differences exert their influences on human abilities via lengthy chains of causes and effects. At any point in the chain an appropriate modification or intervention may eliminate the effect of a difference that might otherwise (indirectly) affect, say, a person's measured intelligence.

The words 'genetic' and 'hereditary' tend to be used interchangeably, but strictly speaking this is wrong. Richard Lewontin (1982) points out that genetic differences are not always inherited. An illustration of this fact is provided by the condition known as Down's syndrome: its cause is a genetic abnormality, but one that is not present in the genes of either parent.

The fact that we are remarkably ignorant concerning the precise nature of genetic influences is a stumbling-block that generates confusion about genetic and environmental contributions to human abilities. Although it is known that genes do have important effects on abilities, very little is understood about the mechanisms or processes by which these effects are exerted. This is important, because in the absence of such knowledge it is difficult to discover whether (and how) it is possible to intervene in ways that compensate for genetic limitations. As was seen in the above example, when that knowledge is available, deciding on appropriate interventions may be a simple matter.

## AREAS OF CONFUSION

Misunderstandings about genetic causation have plagued attempts to discover exactly how hereditary influences actually affect human abilities. It would certainly be absurd to argue that all men and women are created not only equal but identical. But some assertions by psychologists and other scientists who have been at pains to stress the importance of hereditary influences on abilities have been equally absurd, largely because they reflect a faulty understanding of genetics. For instance, the statement that there are 'genes for high intelligence' (Hans Eysenck, in Eysenck versus Kamin, 1981, p. 46), implying that levels of ability are straightforwardly determined by a person's genetic make-up, is inconsistent with an appreciation of the true complexity of genetic mechanisms.

Although it is wrong, the common notion that the inherited and environmental causes of abilities each contribute separately, in an uncomplicated additive manner, is surprisingly persistent. That viewpoint implies that it is reasonable to speak of an ability as being determined to the extent of $x$ per cent by heredity and $y$ per cent by environment, with the sum of $x$ and $y$ being one hundred. But in fact it is wrong to assume that the causes of abilities function in anything like so simple a way. That is obvious as soon as we consider actual causation in the real world, even in things that are much less complex than human abilities.

For example, imagine we were to ask what are the determinants of

he taste of a cake. I doubt that anyone would be very impressed by
an answer that was based on the assumption that, since two of the
eterminants are flour and eggs, we must be able to say that the taste
of a cake depends $x$ per cent on the amount of flour it contains and $y$
er cent on the number of eggs. It would be immediately apparent
that such an approach is ridiculous, largely because it assumes that
the effects of flour and eggs straightforwardly add up, when in fact
the two interact in a complicated way that rules out the possibility of
their contributions being subsequently disentangled. For similar reasons, it would be equally ridiculous to say that, for instance, the
effectiveness of a particular football team was determined to the
extent of $x$ per cent by their speed and $y$ per cent by their accuracy.

The misconception that genetic and environmental causes of abilities simply add together to determine their outcomes underlies a
number of misunderstandings. It is widely assumed that either genetic causes or environmental ones must be more important than the
other, and that the relative strengths of their contributions can be
quantified in a straightforward manner. Another common assumption that is equally mistaken is that if genetic factors are important
then environmental differences between people can have only a weak
influence on their abilities. And, because it is possible to provide
quantitative estimates of the heritability of various traits, some psychologists have been led to believe that there are narrow limits on
what can be achieved by environmental changes.

Measures of heritability can give an indication of the extent to
which a trait has been affected by environmental variability, but
typically in circumstances where such variability is limited, and its
effects underestimated because the crucial variables have not been
accurately measured, or in some instances not even identified
(Lewontin, 1982). Consequently, measures of heritability may fail to
give a realistic indication of the potential potency of environmental
influences.

Some further misconceptions about the outcomes of inheritance are
listed by Richard Lewontin (1982). First, he notes, the belief that
human traits are entirely fixed by genes is quite wrong (although
there are a few exceptions, such as blood group). Even body shape
and rate of metabolism are partly determined by the environment:
Lewontin points out that if one of a pair of identical twins lives at sea
level and does light work, while the other twin spends his life
working in the mountains as a heavy labourer, the two will develop
very different body shapes and metabolic rates.

Another misconception noted by Lewontin is the widely shared belief that genes place firm limits on people's capacities. One common view is that children's abilities are analogous to buckets which can be more or less full (depending on environmental factors) but whose total contents cannot exceed the limitations imposed by the (genetically decided) size of the bucket. He notes that genotypes, unlike buckets, do not in fact have fixed capacities.

Nor, Lewontin insists, is it even correct to say that someone has a genetic tendency to exhibit a particular trait. To illustrate this point, he cites the statement that a certain person has a genetic tendency to be fat, and that in normal environments that person will be fatter than a person with no such genetic tendency. But this assumes that we can specify which environments are 'normal'. Unfortunately, however, we cannot. No one can say that a high or low level of nutrition is normal in human life, or the presence or absence of parasites, or individual competitiveness rather than collective sharing. In a pair of people, the one who is thinner when both of them eat a large amount of food may be fatter than the other when they eat little. Similarly, there are a number of circumstances in which a particular inherited characteristic may lead to a person doing better than someone else under certain environmental conditions, but worse than that person in other conditions.

## INNATE GIFTS AND TALENTS: MYTH AND REALITY

In everyday life people often talk about exceptional individuals in ways that appear to presuppose – in the absence of any evidence at all – that inherited or innate causes must underlie their abilities. To explain why an individual is an exceptional musician, or tennis player, or footballer, someone will say that they have a 'gift' for it, or a 'natural talent', or a special 'aptitude'. Sometimes the individual is said to be 'just gifted', as if that were the end of the matter. The individual has been fortunate enough to be born the recipient of something – a talent, gift, or aptitude – that is the cause of that person's superiority.

If we are to make progress towards a genuine understanding of the causes of exceptional abilities it is vital to appreciate just how flawed that way of thinking actually is. It involves the same kinds of illogical and circular reasoning that we encountered in the previous chapter. The use of terms like 'gifted' in ways that are intended simultaneously to *describe* exceptionally able people and to *explain* their exceptionality can only impede our efforts to understand. This is apparent in the following dialogue:

X: Why do you think Alice is such a good musician?
Y: That's obvious. She has a natural talent [or gift, or aptitude] for it.
X: How do you know she has a natural talent?
Y: That's obvious too. She couldn't possibly be such a wonderful musician unless she had a talent for music.

Here it is clear that Y's thinking turns full circle: a talent or gift is proposed as the cause of something which itself constitutes the only evidence that the talent or gift exists. It is as if I were to state that some inexplicable footprints must have been made by Martians, and, when asked why I am so sure that the Martians were present, reply: 'That's obvious: I've seen their footprints.'

The interchange between X and Y is not a caricature. It is not at all untypical of dialogues I have witnessed on many occasions. If you doubt this, on the next occasion you hear someone describing a young person as having a gift or talent, just try asking the speaker what grounds there are for saying that the individual possesses such a gift or talent. On nine occasions out of ten the reasons given will be the same illogical ones that appear in this dialogue.

## INNATE CAUSES OF VARIATIONS IN ABILITIES: POSSIBLE MECHANISMS

But are gifts and talents necessarily reifications? (See p. 99) Even if it is not logically inevitable that there exists a thing or a quality corresponding to the word 'gift', it may be that there is such a thing or quality, all the same.

For example, consider the following argument. First, when a person is described as being gifted, it is usually fair to say that there is something extraordinary about that person. Second, genetic factors almost certainly contribute, in one way or another, to individual differences in ability. So might it not be legitimate to use the word 'gift' simply to denote whatever genetic causes contribute to the individual's extraordinary qualities?

It would be legitimate to do this, up to a point, but rather misleading. When people speak of, say, 'a gift for music', the implication is that there is some genetic quality which has a specialized musical function. But it might be the case that, on the one hand, exceptional musicians do possess some genetic advantage over other people, but that, on the other hand, this genetic advantage is in no respect specifically musical. For example, perhaps exceptional musicians are genetically advantaged, compared with other people, in having qualities that make them more attentive, more dogged or persistent, or less easily distracted, or in having some distinctive characteristics of personality or temperament that somehow help them to become unusually good at music. In that case, there would indeed be genetic reasons underlying their superior musicianship, but it would be rather misleading to talk of an innate gift for music.

What is important, if it is true that genetic factors contribute to superior abilities, is that we need to know something about the form they take and how they operate. Otherwise, we shall have no way of knowing just how right or wrong we are in asserting that gifts or talents are a cause of superior abilities. So we should try to discover how genetic factors actually contribute to individual variability.

There are a number of possibilities, some more plausible than others. As we shall see, there is a lack of evidence for the existence of the kinds of specific capacity which correspond with most people's idea of an innate gift or talent. But there is evidence that babies do differ, even in the earliest months of life, in ways that in some cases may – indirectly and via a chain of causes and effects – have effects on their eventual patterns of adult abilities.

## 1  SPECIAL COGNITIVE MECHANISMS

The possibility which seems to coincide most closely with popular beliefs about the nature of an innate gift or talent is that certain people are born with cognitive mechanisms or processes that enable them to do things that other people cannot. For instance, the kind of person who becomes an outstanding musician might be someone who has possessed since birth a special mental module or computing system, or special 'music-acquisition device'.

But although it is not totally inconceivable that some people are born with special mental processing mechanisms, the facts suggest otherwise. This possibility can be rejected, because there is absolutely no firm evidence to support it.

## 2  OTHER STRUCTURAL DIFFERENCES

A second possibility is that genetic factors cause fundamental differences in the structure of organs. For instance, inherent differences in muscle structure might conceivably account for variability between people in athletic performance. And if muscular structure affected the flow of blood to the brain, it is possible that performance at mental tasks could also be affected.

Hereditary differences in anatomical structure undoubtedly affect athletic capacity. Different body-builds are more or less advantageous for various sports. But so far as muscles are concerned, research findings indicate that differences in physiological structure may not be innate. It now appears that muscle variables that affect sports performance, such as the relative proportions of different types of muscle, aerobic capacity, and maximum aerobic power, may be only weakly determined by genetic factors. For instance, it is possible that the presence in muscles of a high proportion of slow-twitch fibres, which is associated with athleticism, is largely the result of extended practice at running, rather than the initial cause of differences in ability (Howald, 1982). What is more, it turns out that the differences between athletes and other people in their relative proportions of different muscle fibres are specific to the particular muscles that are exercised in training for an athletic specialization. Kayak racers have unusual proportions of the different fibres in the back muscles, but not in the legs, while the converse is true of runners.

So, while we cannot rule out the possibility that differences in ability are caused by inherent differences in the structure of certain bodily organs, it is important to note that, in some instances at least, research has discovered that structural differences which have long been assumed to be inborn and inherited are in fact the outcome of differences in lifetime experiences.

## 3 INNATE DIFFERENCES IN LEARNING OR MEMORY

Another possibility is that certain people have special innate learning abilities, or special powers of memory. If that were the case, even if it would not be true to say that someone had a gift or talent in the sense of 'a gift for music', it might be reasonable to speak of a person having a gift for learning (or remembering).

But there is no hard evidence that some individuals are inherently exceptional in this way. And, as was pointed out in Chapter 9, learning skills and memory skills are highly specific. The view that some people are good at all memory tasks, or all learning tasks, appears to be mistaken. Performance at many learning and memory tasks is related to ability, but when individuals are assessed at learning or memorizing tasks that are not facilitated by previous learning, individual differences in performance tend to disappear. It is then found that young children may do just as well as adults, and that mentally handicapped people may do just as well as people of normal ability (Belmont, 1978). In those memory tasks which provide no opportunities for experienced people to make effective use of existing knowledge or acquired mental strategies, there is usually no difference in performance between adults and children. In some circumstances young children actually do better than older people (Ceci and Howe, 1978).

In short, it is true that individuals with exceptional abilities are more successful than others at memory and learning tasks that are related to their special expertise, but the superiority is the result, not the cause, of having special skills.

## 4  INHERENT PERCEPTUAL ABILITIES

Perceptual mechanisms are a fourth group of inborn processes that could conceivably act as gifts or talents which make superior achievements possible. For instance, as mentioned in Chapter 7, it has been claimed that some exceptional musicians have been born with the capacity for 'perfect' perception of absolute pitch. This capacity can be a valuable asset for a musician, and a person who possessed it from birth would have an advantage over other would-be musicians.

But investigations have revealed that perfect pitch perception is a learned skill, not an innate ability. It is most often acquired in childhood (Ericsson and Faivre, 1988). Similarly, a number of other unusual perceptual feats that have been widely thought to demand innately special capabilities, including chicken-sexing, certain X-ray diagnostic skills, and various abilities based on the capacity to make delicate discriminations between tastes, smells, and colours, have been found on close examination to be learned skills.

## 5  OTHER PERCEPTUAL DIFFERENCES

Although scientific findings have failed to support the view that some people differ innately from others in having certain specific perceptual capacities that make superior achievements possible, it remains conceivable that there could be some important innate differences in perceptual sensitivity. Such differences, if they exist, might contribute to differences in abilities.

Young infants differ in the amount of sensory stimulation they seem to need (Korner, 1971). Some thrive on a large amount of stimulation: for them, the more stimulation they receive, the better. But others are more sensitive, and are overwhelmed by too much stimulation. These early differences can affect later progress. For instance, because babies gain increased visual stimulation when they are picked up, a child with a strong need for stimulation via the senses will gain considerably from having a mother who picks up her infant unusually frequently. For the same child, the adverse effects of having a mother who neglects to pick her baby up will be very serious. However, for a child who is more visually sensitive, the perceptual outcomes of differing patterns of maternal behaviour will be less extreme. Such a baby will not suffer so much from being picked up relatively infrequently, so far as visual experiences are concerned.

So early differences in perceptual sensitivity may eventually have some influence on later achievements. But the eventual outcomes of such differences are not fixed or direct. Nor are they readily predictable, or irreversible. The actual outcomes also depend on various additional factors, such as the mother's responsiveness and her sensitivity to her infant's preferences. In reality, matters are even more complicated than our example might suggest, since this example concerns only those consequences of picking up an infant that specifically affect vision. A baby will be affected in more than one way by being picked up.

## 6  EARLY DIFFERENCES IN INFANTS' PREFERENCES

Perhaps as a result of very early differences in temperament and in sensitivity to various kinds of sensory information, young children may soon gain preferences for certain kinds of objects and events. Even initially slight preferences can trigger off responses that eventually lead to major differences in a child's competences, by a kind of snowball effect (Renninger and Wozniak, 1985).

At first, a child may simply spend slightly more time observing those objects and events that are preferred. But this may gradually lead to those objects and events being remembered more accurately than non-preferred items, and to higher levels of performance at tasks that involve the preferred objects. In turn, these differences in a child's success, which at this stage may still be quite small, may lead to differences in reinforcement, encouragement, and the feelings that result from doing well at something.

The child may now start to attend more and more selectively to those events which, by this time, are associated with competence and success as well as high levels of interest. By the time a child is 2 or 3 years old the initially small – even quite tiny – variations in preferences may have snowballed into major differences in patterns of competence. By this stage, people who notice that the child has special interests and skills may start to speak of the child as being 'talented' or 'gifted'. And the attention the child receives may further encourage the development of particular competences (which might, for instance, be physical, or musical, or linguistic in form) that adults have remarked on.

## 7 EARLY DIFFERENCES IN TEMPERAMENT AND ACTIVITY LEVEL

These are a seventh and final kind of early differences that might conceivably affect later achievements. If they do, they might be causes of some of the eventual ability differences between people. Innate differences in temperament might conceivably have effects that would justify one person being described as more gifted or talented than others.

Temperamental differences in early infancy do appear to have implications for subsequent development. But, as in the case of early differences in perceptual responsiveness, the long-term consequences of early differences in temperament are not straightforwardly predictable. Moreover, it appears that these differences are by no means unmodifiable: temperament is affected by experiences. For instance, the actions of the child's mother or caretaker can have effects on temperament. It has been established that the consequences of having a particular trait of temperament to an unusually high or low degree are not irreversible (Thomas and Chess, 1979; Dunn, 1979).

How can temperament affect a child's development? One way in which it can depends on the fact that, from a very early age, infants influence their own environments. For instance: if soothed when crying, some babies remain comforted for longer than others; this can influence the mother's reactions – especially if she is inexperienced, her feelings and her self-confidence may be affected by the success or failure of her efforts to comfort the baby; in turn, her own future actions as a mother may be changed.

Mother–infant interactions are also affected by the cuddliness of the child. Anything that influences the nature of such interactions is likely to be important, because the kinds of interaction that occur between a mother and her child have crucial influences on the child's later development. A few infants do not like to be cuddled. They resist their mothers' attempts to hug them, are more restless than others, and dislike physical constraints. Consequently, they have less physical contact with their mothers than other babies, and the interactions that do take place are likely to be atypical, with a variety of possible consequences (Schaffer and Emerson, 1964).

Not all early differences in temperament have long-term effects that can affect abilities, but some almost certainly do. For instance, it is known that unusually active infants tend to become, when they reach the age of 5, children who perform better at physical tasks and at tests measuring verbal achievement. And Sybile Escalona (1973) discovered that infants who are especially sensitive tend to become 5-year-olds who are good at expressing themselves. Even with those early differences of which no obvious trace remains in later years, there is always the possibility that development has been affected in one way or another – an infant's behaviour may, for example, have influenced the parent's behaviour in a way that has been significant in determining the child's progress.

## CONCLUSION

Research investigations have failed to discover any inherited or genetic traits that correspond to the popular notion of a natural gift or talent. Yet it would be totally wrong to conclude that all infants are born identical, so far as the possible precursors of ability differences are concerned. There do exist early differences between infants, some of which are probably inborn and possibly inherited, that can have effects of various kinds on later development. Various types of difference between newborns have consequences that can influence the likelihood of an individual eventually acquiring exceptional abilities. But the outcomes of these early sources of variability are not fixed, or direct, or straightforwardly predictable. The early differences between infants form just one of a large number of interacting factors that, together, help to determine the child's future capabilities.

# FINAL WORDS

The broad aims of this book have included examining various claims concerning the likely benefits and the possible dangers of activities designed to accelerate learning in young children, and giving parents down-to-earth guidance about effective ways to help children master basic skills. There is a substantial amount of evidence (some of which I described in Chapter 2) to support at least some of the claims of those who favour intensive 'hothouse' education for young children. In particular, it is definitely true that ordinary children are capable of gaining certain valuable basic skills much earlier than the vast majority of children normally do. And ordinary parents can do much to help make this possible.

A child can derive great benefit from making good progress towards mastering key abilities such as language. A young child whose language skills are unusually advanced will be better equipped than others to solve many everyday problems. Such a child will be better prepared to learn to read and to profit from the greater independence and the other advantages that reading makes possible. So, while it is wrong to subject young children to regimes of early education that are too formal, narrow, or intense, there is every reason for parents to provide extra opportunities for learning.

To a large extent, the decisions adults make about educating young children depend on their beliefs about the nature and causes of abilities. Many people still believe that the most impressive human accomplishments depend on certain innate talents or gifts. If this were true, the implication would be that the best we can do is identify a child's talents as early as possible and help provide conditions that will nurture them. But that belief belongs to folklore, not science. When we are confronted with the substantial body of findings showing that the majority of children are born capable of acquiring impressive levels of expertise in most spheres of competence, it becomes clear that it is entirely realistic to encourage any normal child to master important basic skills considerably earlier than usual. The advice I have included in the middle chapters of the book will help parents and others to do this.

# REFERENCES

AINSWORTH, M.D.S., BELL, S.M., and STAYTON, D.J. (1974) Infant –mother attachment and social development: socialization as a product of reciprocal responsiveness to signals. In M.P.M. Richards (Ed.) *The Integration of a Child into a Social World*. London: Cambridge University Press.

BAKER, C. (1980) *Reading Through Play: The Easy Way to Teach Your Child*. London: Macdonald Educational.

BELMONT, J. (1978) Individual differences in memory: the cases of normal and retarded development. In M.M. Gruneberg and P.E. Morris (Eds) *Aspects of Memory*. London: Methuen.

BLOOM, B.S. (Ed.) (1985) *Developing Talent in Young People*. New York: Ballantine.

BRADLEY, L. and BRYANT, P.E. (1983) Categorizing sounds and learning to read in preschoolers. *Journal of Educational Psychology, 68*, 680–688.

BRADY, P.T. (1970) The genesis of absolute pitch. *Journal of the Acoustical Society of America, 48*, 883–887.

CECI, S.J., BAKER, J.G., and BRONFENBRENNER, U. (1987) The acquisition of simple and complex algorithms as a function of context. Unpublished manuscript. Ithaca, New York: Cornell University.

CECI, S.J. and HOWE, M.J.A. (1978) Semantic knowledge as a determinant of developmental differences in recall. *Journal of Experimental Child Psychology, 26*, 230–245.

CHASE, W.G. and ERICSSON, K.A. (1981) Skilled memory. In J.R. Anderson (Ed.) *Cognitive Skills and Their Acquisition*. Hillsdale, New Jersey: Erlbaum.

CHASE, W.G. and SIMON, H.A. (1973) Perception in chess. *Cognitive Psychology, 4*, 55–81.

CHI, M.T.H. (1978) Knowledge structures and memory development. In R. Siegler (Ed.) *Children's Thinking: What Develops?* Hillsdale, New Jersey: Erlbaum.

COLES, G. (1987) *The Learning Mystique*. New York: Fawcett Ballantine.

CRYSTAL, D. (1986) *Listen to Your Child*. Harmondsworth: Penguin Books.

CZERNIEWSKA, P. (1985) *How is Language Learned?* (Open University Course E206, Block 2.) Milton Keynes: Open University Press.

DAVIDSON, H.P. (1931) An experimental study of bright, average, and dull children at the four-year mental level. *Genetic Psychology Monographs, 9*, 119–289.

DUNN, J.F. (1979) The first year of life: continuity in individual differences. In D. Shaffer and J.F. Dunn (Eds) *The First Year of Life*. London: Wiley.

DURKIN, D. (1966) *Children Who Read Early*. New York: Teachers College Press, Columbia University.

EINON, D. (1985) *Creative Play*. Harmondsworth: Penguin Books.

ERICSSON, K.A. and FAIVRE, I.A. (1988) What's exceptional about exceptional abilities? In L.K. Obler and D. Fein (Eds) *The Exceptional Brain: Neuropsychology of Talent and Special Abilities*. New York: Guilford Press.

ERICSSON, K.A., TESCH-ROMER, C., AND KRAMPE, R.T. (1990) The role of practice and motivation in the acquisition of expert-level performance in real life: an empirical evaluation of a theoretical framework. In M.J.A.

Howe (Ed.) *Encouraging the Development of Exceptional Abilities and Talents.* Leicester: The British Psychological Society.

ESCALONA, S.K. (1973) The differential impact of environmental conditions as a function of different reaction patterns in infancy. In J.C. Westman (Ed.) *Individual Differences in Children.* New York: Wiley.

EYSENCK, H.J. versus KAMIN, L. (1981) *Intelligence: The Battle for the Mind.* London: Pan Books.

FELDMAN, D.H. (1982) A developmental framework for research with gifted children. In D.H. Feldman (Ed.) *Developmental Approaches to Giftedness and Creativity.* New Directions for Child Development, No. 17. San Francisco: Jossey Bass.

FEUERSTEIN, R. (1980) *Instrumental Enrichment: an Intervention Program for Cognitive Modifiability.* Baltimore: University Park Press.

FORREST, D.W. (1974) *Francis Galton: The Life and Work of a Victorian Genius.* London: Elek.

FOWLER, W. (1983) *Potentials of Childhood. Volume One: A Historical View of Early Experience.* Lexington, Massachusetts: Heath.

FOWLER, W. (1990) Early stimulation and the development of verbal talents. In M.J.A. Howe (Ed.) *Encouraging the Development of Exceptional Abilities and Talents.* Leicester: The British Psychological Society.

FOWLER, W., OGSTON, K., ROBERTS, G., STEANE, D., and SWENSON, A. (1983) *Potentials of Childhood. Volume Two: Studies in Early Developmental Learning.* Lexington, Massachusetts: Heath.

FREEMAN, J. (1990) The intellectually gifted adolescent. In M.J.A. Howe (Ed.) *Encouraging the Development of Exceptional Abilities and Talents.* Leicester: The British Psychological Society.

GARDNER, H. (1984) *Frames of Mind.* London: Heinemann.

GESELL, A. and THOMPSON, H. (1929) Learning and growth in identical infant twins: an experimental study by the method of co-twin control. *Genetic Psychology Monographs,* 6, 1–124.

GOULD, S.J. (1984) *The Mismeasure of Man.* Harmondsworth: Penguin Books.

GUSTIN, W.C. (1985) The development of Olympic swimmers. In B.S. Bloom (Ed.) *Developing Talent in Young People.* New York: Ballantine.

HART, B. and RISLEY, T.R. (1980) *In vivo* language intervention: unanticipated general effects. *Journal of Applied Behaviour Analysis,* 13, 407–432.

HAYES, J.R. (1981) *The Complete Problem Solver.* Philadelphia: The Franklin Institute Press.

HILDESHEIMER, W. (1983) *Mozart.* Translated by M. Faber. London: Dent.

HOWALD, H. (1982) Training-induced morphological and functional changes in skeletal muscle. *International Journal of Sports Medicine,* 3, 1–12.

HOWE, M.J.A. (1982) Biographical evidence and the development of outstanding individuals. *American Psychologist,* 37, 1071–1081.

HOWE, M.J.A. (1989) *Fragments of Genius: The Strange Feats of Idiots Savants.* London: Routledge.

HOWE, M.J.A. (1990) *The Origins of Exceptional Abilities.* Oxford: Blackwell.

HUNT, J. McV. (1986) The effect of variations in quality and type of early child care on development. In W. Fowler (Ed.) *Early Experience and the Development of Competence.* New Directions for Child Development, No. 32. San Francisco: Jossey Bass.

KALINOWSKI, A.G. (1985) The development of Olympic swimmers. In B.S.

Bloom (Ed.) *Developing Talent in Young People*. New York: Ballantine.
KOLATA, G. (1984) Studying in the womb. *Science, 225*, 302–303.
KOLDENER, W. (1970) *Antonio Vivaldi: His Life and Work*. Translated by W. Hopkins. London: Faber & Faber.
KORNER, A.F. (1971) Individual differences at birth: implications for early experience and later development. *American Journal of Orthopsychiatry, 41*, 608–619.
KUNKEL, J.H. (1985) Vivaldi in Venice: an historical test of psychological propositions. *Psychological Record, 35*, 445–457.
LEWIS, D. (1976) Observations on route-finding and spatial orientation among the aboriginal peoples of the western desert region of central Australia. *Oceania, 46*, 249–282.
LEWONTIN, R. (1982) *Human Diversity*. New York: Freeman.
McCABE, A. (1987) *Language Games to Play with Your Child*. New York: Fawcett Columbine.
McGRAW, M. (1935) *Growth: A Study of Johnny and Jimmy*. New York: Appleton-Century-Crofts.
McGRAW, M. (1939) Later development of children specially trained during infancy: Johnny and Jimmy at school age. *Child Development, 10*, 1–19.
MEAD, M. (1975) *Growing Up in New Guinea*. New York: William Morrow.
MENYUK, P. (1977) *Language and Maturation*. Cambridge, Mass: MIT Press.
METZL, M.N. (1980) Teaching parents a strategy for enhancing infant development. *Child Development, 51*, 583–586.
MILL, J.S. (1971) *Autobiography*. London: Oxford University Press. (Originally published in 1873.)
MONSAAS, J.A. (1985) The development of Olympic swimmers. In B.S. Bloom (Ed.) *Developing Talent in Young People*. New York: Ballantine.
NELSON, K. (1977) Facilitating children's syntax acquisition. *Developmental Psychology, 13*, 101–107.
NELSON, K., CARSKADDON, G., and BONVILLIAN, J.D. (1973) Syntax acquisition: impact of experimental variation in adult verbal interaction with the child. *Child Development, 44*, 497–504.
PACKE, M.StJ. (1954) *The Life of John Stuart Mill*. London: Secker & Warburg.
PETERSEN, G.A. and SHERROD, K.B. (1982) Relationship of maternal language to language development and language delay of children. *American Journal of Mental Deficiency, 86*, 391–398.
RADFORD, J. (1990) *Child Prodigies and Exceptional Early Achievement*. Brighton: Harvester Press.
RENNINGER, K.A. and WOZNIAK, R.N. (1985) Effect of interest on attentional shift, recognition and recall in young children. *Developmental Psychology, 21*, 624–632.
SCHAFFER, H.R. and EMERSON, P.E. (1964) Patterns of response to physical contact in early human development. *Journal of Child Psychology and Psychiatry, 5*, 1–13.
SLOANE, K.D. (1985) Home influences on talent development. In B.S. Bloom (Ed.) *Developing Talent in Young People*. New York: Ballantine.
SLOANE, K.D. and SOSNIAK, L.A. (1985) The development of accomplished sculptors. In B.S. Bloom (Ed.) *Developing Talent in Young People*. New York: Ballantine.

SLOBODA, J.A. (1985) *The Musical Mind: The Cognitive Psychology of Music.* London: Oxford University Press.

SOSNIAK, L.A. (1985) Learning to be a concert pianist. In B.S. Bloom (Ed.) *Developing Talent in Young People.* New York: Ballantine.

SOSNIAK, L.A. (1990) The tortoise, the hare, and the development of talent. In M.J.A. Howe (Ed.) *Encouraging the Development of Exceptional Abilities and Talents.* Leicester: The British Psychological Society.

STAATS, A.W. (1971) *Child Learning, Intelligence, and Personality.* New York: Harper & Row.

THOMAS, A. and CHESS, S. (1979) *Temperament and Development.* New York: Brunner-Mazel.

VALDEZ-MENCHACA, M.C. and WHITEHURST, G.J. (1988) The effects of incidental teaching on vocabulary acquisition by young children. *Child Development*, 59, 1451–1459.

WALLACE, A. (1986) *The Prodigy: A Biography of William James Sidis, the World's Greatest Child Prodigy.* London: Macmillan.

WALMSLEY, J. and MARGOLIS, J. (1987) *Hot House People: Can We Create Super Human Beings?* London: Pan Books.

WHITE, B.L. (1971) *Human Infants: Experience and Psychological Development.* Englewood Cliffs, New Jersey: Prentice-Hall.

WHITE, B.L. (1985) Competence and giftedness. In J. Freeman (Ed.) *The Psychology of Gifted Children.* Chichester: Wiley.

WHITEHURST, G.J., FALCO, F.L., LONIGAN, C.J., FISCHEL, J.E., De-BARYSHE, B.D., VALDEZ-MENCHACA, M.C., and CAULFIELD, M. (1988) Accelerating language development through picture book reading. *Developmental Psychology*, 24, 552–559.

WIENER, H.S. (1988) *Talk With Your Child.* New York: Viking Penguin.

WIENER, N. (1953) *Ex-Prodigy: My Childhood and Youth.* New York: Simon & Schuster.

YOUNG, P. and TYRE, C. (1985) *Teach Your Child to Read.* London: Fontana.

# INDEX